Praise for

At the Crossroads

... each of us."

—NICHOLE NORDEMAN, songwriter and recording artist

"Before reading [Charlie's] thoughts, I knew I was stirred by some Christian music, turned off by some, and indifferent to much. Now my appetite is whetted for what God can do through music within the surprising boundaries he draws and Charlie describes. A compelling, thoughtful discussion of music's power to be truly spiritual."

    —LARRY CRABB JR., author of *The Pressure's Off*

"Charlie Peacock has written the definitive book on today's music and the church. Though the names and thoughts of stars dot its pages, it is the Holy Spirit–inspired, Scripture-based insights that grab and compel."

    —THE LATE BOB BRINER, author of *Roaring Lambs*

"When it comes to matters of faith, popular culture, and music, Charlie Peacock is like my mother: If we disagree, chances are she's right and I'm wrong. Charlie knows the terrain of the faith-based music world and deftly explores the theological underpinnings that created a world in which Christians who played popular music ended up singing almost exclusively for fellow believers. But he doesn't just criticize; he offers a way out so that the music made by people of faith can be enjoyed by all music fans."

    —MARK JOSEPH, author of *Faith, God and Rock 'n' Roll*

"As someone who daily works with 'Christian artists,' I constantly ask and answer questions about this Christian music industry. *At the Crossroads* is a thorough analysis for anyone who has found him- or herself a part of the confusing and seemingly endless Christian music debate."

—CHRISTOPHER YORK, director A&R, EMI CMG Label Group

"Bravo! If Charlie Peacock is pointing fingers, it's not at the Christian music industry but to the holy light that can transform it."

—LOU CARLOZO, *Chicago Tribune*

"*At the Crossroads* is a sincere plea for honest reflection and critical assessment of contemporary Christian music. Charlie Peacock calls for a new vision, a 'comprehensive kingdom perspective' as a guide through the labyrinth of hype, conformity, worldliness, and anti-intellectualism that has plagued the enterprise."

—WILLIAM D. ROMANOWSKI, Calvin College, author of *Eyes Wide Open*

"Charlie Peacock's book is an honest, informed, and passionate critique of how evangelicals have created a musical ghetto grounded in thin theology, polluted piety, cultural claustrophobia, and corporate confusion. Every believer ought to read it, weep, and then take up Peacock's challenge to find a better way to transform worldwide culture for the God of the universe."

—QUENTIN J. SCHULTZE, Calvin College, author of *Internet for Christians*

"Charlie Peacock does an amazing job of discussing the pervading questions asked by today's Christian music artist and listener."

—SHAWN YOUNG, CCM Department, Greenville College

"A refreshing and challenging book for any Christian seriously engaged in the creative process."

—PEGGY WEHMEYER, Religion Correspondent, ABC News

Inside the Past, Present, and Future
of Contemporary Christian Music

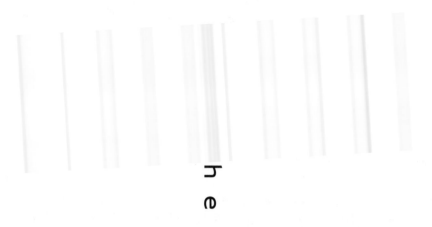

Charlie Peacock
with Molly Nicholas

foreword by Steven Curtis Chapman
afterword by Jars of Clay

SHAW BOOKS
an imprint of WATERBROOK PRESS

At the Crossroads
A SHAW BOOK
PUBLISHED BY WATERBROOK PRESS
2375 Telstar Drive, Suite 160
Colorado Springs, Colorado 80920
A division of Random House, Inc.

At the Crossroads was previously released in an earlier edition by Broadman & Holman Publishers under the same title.

ISBN 0-87788-128-6

Copyright © 2004 by Charlie Peacock-Ashworth

The Library of Congress has cataloged the hardcover edition as follows:
Peacock, Charlie.
At the crossroads : an insider's look at the past, present, and future of contemporary Christian music / by Charlie Peacock.
    p. cm.
  ISBN 0-8054-1822-9 (hardcover)
    1. Contemporary Christian music—History and criticism. I. Title.
ML3187.5P37 1998
782.25—dc21   98-43996

Printed in the United States of America
2004

10 9 8 7 6 5 4 3 2 1

Contents

Acknowledgments—Original Edition

...important. Thanks and appreciation to Steve Turner, who was there before I arrived. Dan Russell—you were a great encouragement to me in those early years as well.

Many thanks to Billy Ray Hearn, Bill Hearn, and all the folks at EMI Christian Music Group, especially Peter York, who became my musical champion in 1989 and carefully ushered me into the full embrace of the Christian music community. Brown Bannister, you were there too. Thanks.

Thank you, Scotty Smith, for your teaching and for the Art House years. To all those who supported the AH mission, especially Nick Barré, Doug McKelvey, Jay Swartzendruber, Russ Ramsey, David Dark, Christ Community Church, and all the students, financial supporters, and volunteers—thanks. It was good.

Special mention must be given to Dr. Leland Ryken, who first suggested I write this book, as well as to Edith Schaeffer and Frederick Buechner, who both sent words of encouragement in the early days of the Art House. Glenn Kaiser and JPUSA, Andy and Sue Boyer—you were there as well. Thank you.

To R. C. Sproul, R. C. Jr, Dick and Mardi Keyes, Quentin Schultze, William Romanowski, Michael Horton, Os Guinness—thank you for your teaching and your encouragement. Ken Hefner—keep up the good work.

I owe a huge debt of thanks to the kind people who have supported my music throughout the years. Thank you for caring and for saying so. I'm privileged to walk in community with you.

To Molly Ashworth Nicholas, April Hefner, and Greg Rumburg (all gifted writers)—thank you for figuring the statistics, proofreading during the early stages of the book, and offering helpful suggestions. Len Goss—thank you for sweeping the tangential under the rug. Wes Yoder—thank you for guarding the vision. Mike Butera—thank you for your obedience in telling me the truth; it set me free. Thank you, SCC and Jars, for your faithfulness. Many thanks to all the artists who participated in the interviews. Respect to the pioneers of CCM.

To my son Sam and to my new son Mark Nicholas—this book is for you both. You're the future of the music. Choose well.

To my wife and best friend, Andi—I love you so much. Thank you for your great patience and for not letting me quit when I wanted to. Kiss me like a...

A final word of thanks to my friend and mentor Bob Briner, who has championed me since the moment we met. I could not have written this book without you, Bob. Knowing you has helped make me a better man. You make the invisible kingdom visible.

ACKNOWLEDGMENTS—REVISED AND UPDATED EDITION

Thank you, Molly Nicholas and Elisa Fryling Stanford, for your invaluable help in preparing this new version of *At the Crossroads*. If it is more readable and informative than the first version, it's because you excel at all you put your hands and hearts to. Don Pape—you wrangled another one out of me, and for that I'm grateful. You are a publisher extraordinaire.

A Note from the Author on Terminology

or Handel's *Messiah*? Or are we talking about Charles Tindley and Tommy Dorsey? Or are we talking about all of it, from the psalms of King David to dc Talk? What about gospel music? What about Southern gospel? What about black gospel? Why all the gospels? You can see the challenge here.

I knew I wanted to write about something that happened with Christians and music starting back in the late '60s—something that today is a five-hundred-million-dollar-a-year industry. And though it has included black gospel and Southern gospel, and even some Gregorian chants, the music and industry I needed to put a name on had always been more about a kind of Christianized pop/rock music—music that changes with the pop music of the surrounding culture. This music and the community of artists, industry workers, and audience members it represents are usually referred to today as "contemporary Christian music," or CCM for short. Though many of the music's earliest pioneers perpetuated this terminology (and derivations of it), a magazine called *Contemporary Christian Music/CCM* set the name in stone and has continued to help refine its meaning for more than twenty-five years.

CCM is a registered trademark of Salem Communications, home to *CCM Magazine*, a Christian radio network, and other enterprises important to the nurture and growth of this unique musical form. It is with the kind permission of *CCM Magazine* founder John Styll that I make use of the CCM acronym throughout the pages that follow. This permission does not in any way indicate an endorsement of *At the Crossroads* by *CCM Magazine* or Salem Communications. In addition, the opinions expressed in *At the Crossroads* by this author or any other parties do not necessarily reflect the opinions of *CCM Magazine* or Salem Communications.

Foreword

...to find a pen and a piece of paper to write down those lyrics?

Undoubtedly, the message of Jesus's parable in Matthew 25, commonly called the parable of the talents, awakened a new passion in me. This parable tells the story of several servants who are entrusted by their master with certain "talents" to be used in a way that would honor him and show good stewardship. In pondering this story, I was struck with a deep desire to simulate the "good and faithful servant" who heard those treasured words of his master: "Well done." After a few hours with my guitar and a trash can filled with crumpled sheets of paper, I emerged with the first of my many musical "cries of the heart," which I hoped would be pronounced, "Well done." While this wouldn't prove to be my most creatively crafted song, it was as sincere a lyric as I have ever penned, and I have referred to it many times throughout the years as my mission statement on the art that God has allowed me to share. It read:

Before he left this earth for heaven, Jesus commanded us to go
And bring all people to him, by letting His love through us show.
When Christ comes I just want to hear Him say
When Christ comes I just want to hear Him say "Well done."

At the tender age of fifteen, I had little notion of the significance of Christ's challenge. What would it really mean to live in such a way that he would be able to say those words to me: "Well done, good and faithful servant"? Now, twenty years later, I am still considering the implications of that parable, and that is why I think the book you are holding in your hand is so important.

To think that Almighty God would give us the sacred trust of the message of reconciliation and send us out as ambassadors through whom his appeal would be made is a truth that should humble and astonish us (2 Corinthians 5:19-20). And when we realize that the Artist and Creator of all things has invited us into the creative process and entrusted us with unique artistic abilities to use for his glory, we should truly feel awed and yet sobered by a sense of our own responsibility and need for wisdom.

I know of no one who has wrestled more profoundly with these issues and how they relate to the arts, especially Christian music, than Charlie Peacock. I can't help but think how invaluable a book like this would have been to me as I took my first steps in serving my Master by using the gifts and abilities he has given me. The relationship between the importance of theology and the goals of Christian music is alone worth the time invested in reading this book.

This book does not answer all of our questions about Christian music and how it should be "done." Instead, it allows the Holy Spirit to guide us to solutions, however different and unique they may be. I believe God will use it in the lives of his children, like you and me, who are "compelled by the love of Christ" to use our gifts and talents in such a way that our Master might say, "Well done, good and faithful servant."

—STEVEN CURTIS CHAPMAN

Preface to the Revised and Updated Edition

_____ ___ ___ important topic. This being so, it is likely that I will return to this topic again and again."

It is with six more years of joys, disappointments, epiphanies, anxieties, biblical study, and, hopefully, wisdom under my belt that I revisit this book that represents the culmination of more than twenty years of conversations, observations, and experience as a musician and a student-follower of Jesus.

Much of what I've been learning about what it means to be a follower of Jesus and how it relates to the whole of life can be found in my book *New Way to Be Human.* For this updated and revised edition of *At the Crossroads,* I turn once again to the subject of music, specifically what has historically been known as contemporary Christian music (CCM), and the cultural and musical changes that surround it. Throughout the book I will leave the use of the abbreviation CCM intact, though it is worth noting that the word *contemporary* is seldom used anymore. As of this writing the words *Christian music* enjoy more use, especially in the media (outside the Christian community).

In the span of six years, much has changed in the music industry at large, including in CCM. As is the case at any given time in this industry, some of the artists who are now at the top are different than those who were there several years before. Some who were performing in small youth camps are now playing ten-thousand-seat arenas, and vice versa. Some artists who are now at the top of the charts were still in high school when the first edition of this book was released.

Other significant and perhaps less predictable changes have occurred in CCM in recent years. What is categorized as "worship music" has seen unprecedented sales and popularity. With the rise of the Internet, we've also seen changes in the way people purchase music—or obtain it without paying for it. Whereas the Christian music industry was at a financial peak several years ago, the current concern of many record labels today is mere survival. But the most significant change is in musicians' attitudes toward the system of CCM as a means of marketing and delivery for their art making. As a result, many of the best and brightest artists who profess to take Jesus seriously are abandoning the CCM industry—not even considering it as a mechanism for getting their music out to people. After many years of producing recordings for the system, I clearly understand why they would make this choice.

As for me, I have not completely abandoned making music for followers of Jesus—the Christian church. There are still compelling reasons to link up with individuals in the CCM industry, on a case-by-case basis, to attempt good, God-honoring work to foster authentic community. It would be difficult for me to ever abandon that mission; it seems to me to be deeply connected to what it means to be human. Still, I've reached the point where I take such issue with the creation and cultivation of "Christian music" as a genre that I'm conflicted when I do contribute. If nothing else, this book is me wrestling with the conflict, looking for solutions, looking for light.

Thankfully, this is a time for new ideas and approaches to the distribution and promotion of music. As a result, most of my work is now carried out in the arena where I began my musical and spiritual journey: the realm of popular music. With my renewed focus on pop music has also come a renewal of imagination and creative freedom—a much needed one in fact. Given what Christians profess to believe about reality (that humans are made to image God in creativity and holiness), it's odd that pop music would be a much freer and open venue for imagination and creativity than so-called Christian music.

But this is the strange world and time we live in. I still dream of a future time when people who profess to follow Jesus will actually lead culture rather than follow.

It's like h...

...language to be informative and welcoming to any and all readers. Where I have failed in this endeavor, I ask for your patience and forgiveness.

Introduction

with the devil, and Robert [Johnson] claimed to have struck such a deal."[1]

In the book of Matthew, we read about Jesus at a crossroads. The devil came to him while he was fasting in the desert. The Scriptures tell us that Satan led Jesus up to a mountaintop and showed him all the kingdoms of the world in all their splendor. Then the devil offered to strike a deal with him, saying, "All this I will give you...if you will bow down and worship me." Jesus refused, saying, "Away from me, Satan! For it is written: 'Worship the Lord your God, and serve him only' " (Matthew 4:9-10).

As it was for Robert Johnson and Jesus, so it is for the men and women of contemporary Christian music (CCM). The crossroads is always about choosing between the kingdoms of the world and the kingdom of God. For CCM it's also about choosing between subjective ideas that have to do with music, the church, and the culture, and God's objective kingdom ideas concerning these same things. Positively speaking, the crossroads represents the opportunity for followers of Jesus to begin to approach music, ministry, and, yes, industry in a far more comprehensive and faithful manner. By "faithful," I mean that our ways of being, speaking, knowing, and doing are congruent with God's desire for humanity—that they are in keeping with the ways of Jesus.

While some Christians believe that CCM is controlled by the devil and his evil spirits, I for one do not. I know of no CCM legend or lore that tells of a Christian musician who sold his soul to the devil for talent, fame, or fortune. What I do know is that all human endeavor is problematic, and no Christian enterprise is beyond the stain of sin and failure. Are there problems we need to address at this crossroads? Yes, there are many, and this book addresses them head-on.

I'm aware that for every problem and example of poor stewardship of talent and resources, remarkable exceptions do exist, and for these faithful exceptions I'm grateful. Perhaps you're one of them. With this admission in mind, I kindly ask that as you read this book, you would look past my use of generalizations to the very real problems these generalizations seek to expose. I desire to write as a peacemaker, not a troublemaker. A peacemaker reconciles people to the Jesus way of being and doing. It is fidelity to his kingdom ways that drives both book and writer. My aim is to stress the word and work of God as revealed in the Bible. It isn't to dress down people who have erred or with whom I am not in agreement. Borrowing words from Eugene Peterson, I pray that my writing will reveal me not as a "bystander criticizing" or a "turncoat propagandizing," but rather as an "insider agonizing."[2] As it has been said, "He has the right to criticize who has the heart to help." I have the heart to help.

Compass Check

Christian music is at a crossroads between what was and is, and what's yet to come. This book is a compass check, a way of setting aside time to look back, assess where the music is, and most important, choose a true and faithful future direction. As a follower of Jesus, I have a vested interest in seeing that we choose our direction faithfully. I believe that books ought to be written for the benefit of people and communities, and this book—or compass check— is no exception. All along I've imagined it being of benefit to anyone and everyone connected with contemporary Christian music: artists, industry, and audience. I have hoped that professors, teachers, parents, youth workers, and pastors would find it helpful as well. I have tried to write in such a way that young musicians just starting out might find answers to their many questions, regardless of whether they use their talents in church, Christian music or the mainstream pop music business

pop music and the Christian music industry. I secured my first major label artist development deal with A&M Records in 1980 and went on to make recordings for Exit, A&M, Island, and Sparrow. As a record producer I have had the privilege of working with many talented artists including the 77s, Avalon, Margaret Becker, Ladysmith Black Mambazo, Out of the Grey, Al Green, Sarah Masen, Rich Mullins, Michael Card, CeCe Winans, Twila Paris, Audio Adrenaline, Nichole Nordeman, Sara Groves, and Switchfoot. More than 250 songs I've either written or cowritten have been recorded by artists in Christian and pop music. In addition to the callings of artist, producer, and songwriter, I have also experienced the joy and challenge of founding my own record label, re:think. All told, there is little concerning the music business in general or Christian music specifically that I have not experienced, and it is from this experience that I have written this book.

THE PURPOSE OF THIS BOOK

This book could easily have been devoted to recounting the tremendous good that has come from Christian music—a volume jam-packed with testimonies from artists, audience, and industry. But such a book, I believe, would have been premature and arguably less helpful to those wanting to understand the real issues confronting CCM. Despite what some critics report, significant good has come of CCM, and God has received glory and honor and praise as a result. Even so, I cannot stress too strongly that the mission of this particular book is not to tell the long history of CCM or to testify to the good necessarily. The primary purpose of this book is to explain the need for repentance, rethinking, and reimagining despite evidence of jewels scattered among the dross.

My intention is first to isolate from CCM's historical beginnings those theologies and ideologies that have shaped and influenced artists, industry, and audience demonstrably more than all the others. Then I will discuss how these powerful and enduring ideas have essentially formed an ad hoc philosophy of Christian music, informing and defining CCM artistry, industry, and audience from the beginning to the present. Throughout the book I try to respectfully and lovingly critique these notions, making clear that these foundational theologies, philosophies, and ideologies do not accurately reflect a comprehensive kingdom perspective or the whole story of the Jesus way and mission—a story that the CCM community is called to step into with intentionality and faithfulness.

Throughout this book I often mention a comprehensive kingdom perspective as well as the human mission Jesus has given his people. While both of these concepts will be explored in more detail later, I will give a brief description of each here. First, a *comprehensive kingdom perspective* refers to the ability to see life as God sees it (as much as is humanly possible). This phrase is very much akin to a *biblical worldview*—a way of thinking about life and the world that is informed by the Scriptures. Second, the *human mission* denotes those activities to which God has called his people—specifically, telling the Story of God, people, and place, loving our neighbors, doing acts of mercy, and managing the creation he left us in charge of.

The people who make up the CCM community have an undeniable zeal and love for Christ. To me this is beyond debate. But it is my opinion that although our intentions are often exemplary, the foundational ideas and methods that started CCM and continue to fuel much of it today are incomplete and, as such, fail to provide CCM participants with a sufficient theological or ideological foundation from which to create music, ministry, and industry.

...ng. It is, instead, to accurately identify where we are in order to discern which direction is forward. This information is important and helpful to have when you're standing at the crossroads. My hope is that this kind of in-depth analysis will give those of us who haven't found what we're looking for at the intersection of Christian faith, music, and the music business the necessary ammunition with which to battle apathy, complacency, and unwanted conformity.

Like most organizational systems, CCM promotes conformity. Some conformity and bias is built into the system and is necessary to its survival. Healthy conformity within a system produces an ordered and stable environment where good can flourish. For example, conforming to many of the conventions of business helps a person or company stay in business and make a profit. And profit at its best can be used to contribute to the good of others.

However, another kind of conformity that is not good is conformity born of fear and lack of faith in God. It produces legalism, performance-based acceptability, and stunted, uninspired imaginations. Wherever an abundance of this kind of conformity exists, there is little room for diverse, faithful, and imaginative business, music, and the care of people and place. Unfortunately, this type of conformity is also found in CCM.

Conformity to some standard provides the foundation for imaginative growth. Creation conforms to certain norms and conventions, and yet it does so without taking away from its astonishing diversity. But conformity that cultivates more conformity, season after season, is antihuman, anticreation, and, ultimately, antikingdom. The CCM community would do well to take its cues from the model of God's creativity.

CCM AND THE EVANGELICAL CULTURE

CCM mirrors the culture of the evangelical church from which it was launched some thirty plus years ago. Like those immersed in evangelicalism, the CCM community is a fragmented lot composed of special-interest groups. Each special-interest group is fueled by a particular theological/ideological bias or denominational/nondenominational connection that affects its thinking. Some of these special-interest groups act out of obedience to the doctrine of the body of Christ. In other words, they know and understand that they have been set apart to do a unique work specific to their musical calling. Because of this, they respect those who've been called to something altogether different from them. They work in loving cooperation with their brothers and sisters and do not tear down their different but equally important work.

Other special-interest groups are not so healthy. Some believe that they alone model the way authentic Christian music ought to be done. Often the ideas and positions held by these groups are reinforced not so much by a kingdom perspective or a biblical way of thinking as by the vote of the Christian at the cash register, the ticket counter, and, unfortunately, even the altar. In other words, the more positive votes a special-interest group can acquire, the more justified its members feel in taking a particular position regarding Christian music. Even though this kind of market-driven view of success can produce a certain arrogance, a lack of votes is no guarantee of humility. Some special-interest groups rationalize the failure to secure support for their position and methods by maintaining that their particular spin on Christian music is so right and powerful that the enemy is fighting to keep it from the people.

The presence of this type of uncharitable separatist position within the larger CCM community works against achieving anything other than the narrowest consensus as to what Christian music is. Instead of having an ocean of possibilities

g to the image of Jesus will we have eyes to see the diverse purposes that music created by followers of Jesus can and should have.

My intent is to stir within you a desire for the truth in all things, not necessarily to convert you to my point of view. Along the way, if you do become convinced that a position I've taken is truthful, then choose it freely, as one who is convinced, not coerced. Above all, seek the truth, and settle for nothing less. There is a way of thinking that accepts as true what feels right, or what works or gets the job done. In this way of thinking, subjectivism and pragmatism replace the requirement and glorious freedom of thinking and living according to God's revealed truth. Christians who live under this truth requirement live in the light of a controlling narrative in which feelings and methods are held up to the bright light of God's Word. Checking our feelings and methods against the sure Word of God is a full-time activity for Christians who are serious about taking hold of the life that is truly the kingdom life. This is, in fact, an activity that defines us. Consider J. I. Packer's words:

> What is a Christian?… He is a man who acknowledges and lives under the word of God. He submits without reserve to the word of God written in "the Scripture of truth" (Daniel 10:21), believing the teaching, trusting the promises, following the commands.[3]

ON PROBLEMS AND SOLUTIONS

For many readers, I suspect this book will offer a new way of looking at Christian music and, beyond that, at life in general. Though it's necessary to face the problems in CCM head-on, this book is also about proposing solutions. In addition to listening to and analyzing the critical and exuberant voices within our community, I endeavor to offer solutions to the problems that these voices have brought to our attention. Second, I offer solutions to problems that are, frankly, seldom identified as problems in CCM. Last of all, I offer my own ideas about the future direction of a community at the crossroads.

For some readers, the problems I address will articulate what they have always suspected but may not have put into words. My hope is that the solutions I've proposed will, for many readers, closely represent their own good dreams for music, or at least offer a starting place from which we can together rethink and reimagine "Christian" music. Others may be disappointed to find that the problems they perceive to be the most critical and the solutions they thought obvious have been played down or are missing altogether. This is the inevitable outcome of writing a book that is not meant to be an exhaustive study of its subject.

Throughout the book you will notice that I emphasize the need for those involved and interested in CCM to do the following:

1. Recover a comprehensive knowledge of the Story of God, people, and place to the end that we know and understand God's thoughts about himself as well as his thoughts about his creation, his kingdom at hand, and his kingdom that is to come.

2. Renew our love for God and begin to live in response to his grace in every sphere of our existence, from prayer and praise to music making and marketing.

3. Recover the human mission defined as follows:

a. Living out the word and work of Jesus so that people see it is a true
and better way to be human, and so that those who are already following will become more and more interested in the things Jesus is

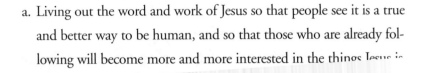

people in
God's place under God's rule or ways—and make life choices based
on this perspective.

The future direction of Christian music is in the hands of the people who
decide for it—the artists, the industry leaders, and the audience. For some, the
crossroads will be a time of assessment, repentance, and renewed dedication to
God's kingdom purposes. For others it will be a time of scrambling, positioning, and deal making. The direction we decide to take at the crossroads, today
or in the days to come, will ultimately be determined by what we understand
our calling to be and what we know and understand of God's kingdom.

Initially, the idea of repentance as well as rethinking and reimagining
CCM could garner tremendous support from artists, industry, and audience.
Yet because CCM is now so fragmented (having less and less consensus as to
its mission) and so individualistic (having less and less of a sense of the body
of Christ working together), we should expect the idea to lose its appeal when
it affects personal and corporate financial scenarios or challenges deeply held
presuppositions about the purpose and work of CCM. Even if your own study
of the biblical Story proves to you that the problems in CCM are authentic
and change is needed, fear of others and the love of money and self can easily
steal the desire to embrace the solutions and future direction you know are
right. Only a love for God and a fearful reverence for him can empower any

of us to respond to the Holy Spirit with an authentic desire to let go of our fears, our worldliness, and our pride.

Since 1982 I have been thinking about what it means to be a musician and a follower of Jesus. You now hold in your hands my sincerest and most heartfelt thoughts on the subject of contemporary Christian music after more than two decades of serving God and my community as a musician. Keep in mind that this book is mostly about this strange occurrence in history called contemporary Christian music. It is not necessarily a book about music and followers of Jesus, which would be another subject altogether and would fill many, many books. Still, on the subject at hand, I have prayed to write with grace, charity, and an overriding concern and love for others. Where I have missed the mark, I humbly ask my reader's forgiveness.

For some readers, tackling this book will represent a first effort at really thinking this subject through. Don't be afraid to take it in bite-sized chunks or to skip around. Since this book delivers a dual theological message, one for life and, simultaneously, one for Christian music, I would imagine readers returning to this book and to various chapters (paragraphs even) at different seasons of their lives.

I'm aware that much of this book is very philosophical. It's not a tell-all exposé of Christian music, and it's not a how-to book. It's a book that is meant to encourage faithful responses to the relentless grace of God in the world. It does not concern me whether good comes from your reading just one chapter or the whole book. May good come. That's what matters.

Spirit, come flush out the lies. Bring truth. Help us to repent, to rethink, to reimagine, and to choose well for the future. Help me, the neediest, most of all.

From modest beginnings in the 1960s, contemporary Christian music (CCM) has grown exponentially both as a business and as a ministry. In the 1990s Christian music enjoyed what was at that point unprecedented popularity and success. Sales of popular Christian music increased dramatically, from thirty-three million units sold in 1996 to forty-four million units in 1997. The '90s also saw Christian artists like Amy Grant, Bob Carlisle, dc Talk, Jars of Clay, and Kirk Franklin garner hit singles and albums in the mainstream marketplace. Though the rate of increase in sales has slowed down in the twenty-first century, the Christian music industry is still selling close to fifty million albums a year. And we are still seeing artists like Stacie Orrico, P.O.D., MercyMe, and Switchfoot find popularity with both Christian and mainstream audiences.

Given this kind of success over the years, what is there to imply that contemporary Christian music is at a crossroads?

Despite the fact that some in the CCM community and audience are disturbed by the business side of CCM and its quest for financial profit, and others, particularly industry executives, are alarmed by the leveling or declining sales figures of recent years, I do not believe that cash flow is the problem. The problem is with the spiritual foundation of a musical form that is completely dependent on that foundation for artistic direction and ultimate commercial

CCM's musical foundation is formed wrong

success. In addition, artists, promoters, record companies, radio stations, and millions of listeners are deeply divided over the purpose of CCM, its mission, and even its definition.

As the Cheshire Cat told Alice in Wonderland, "When you don't know where you're going, any road will do." Until we lock onto a God-breathed direction for our music, we're stuck in the middle of the intersection, tapping our feet. Spiritually, we're at the most important crossroads in the history of the industry.

A DIN OF VOICES

Contemporary Christian music is filled with the sound of many voices offering opinions and shouting questions. Like the music of the church throughout the ages, CCM is subject to the criticism of the church and the culture. For many Christians, CCM is a blessing—a gift from God. For some, it's an embarrassment. Others have never heard of it. CCM fans, parents, teachers, cultural critics, pastors and priests, people eager to be a part of the CCM community, and gifted young artists committed to taking their music to an unbelieving culture—all are looking for answers.

Many simply want to know where Jesus fits in amid all the show-biz buzz and hype. In response to this kind of questioning, record companies spend a good deal of time and money to assure listeners that Jesus is at the heart of both the music and the artists they promote.

Others argue that CCM is nothing but vapid Christian subculture clichés set to the beat of what they term "secular" culture. Often their mission is to redirect CCM lovers back to the riches of hymnody and to warn their listeners and readers that CCM is substandard and trivial. Others are even less charitable. For them CCM is nothing short of the devil's handiwork. As one Christian mother has said, "You will never convince me that this [CCM] is of the Lord."[1]

Which road leads to the truth?

Over the last several years, the CCM community has addressed key issues in various public forums to a greater extent than at any time in its thirty-five-year history—issues such as the near-wholesale buyout of Christian record companies by mainstream corporations and the debat

lyric "Christian" and anoth

plague

....cu Christ? Who and what are

..., are not imaginary voices. They are the voices of real people—people wanting to be heard.

The *voices of criticism* are those that simply cannot affirm CCM as it is presently constituted. Their criticism is meant to lead the CCM community to greater faithfulness. Other voices say CCM has drifted so far from the shore of truth that it's time to abandon the cursed ship. Still other voices come from critics outside the church.

If we listen further we'll hear *voices of debate* wrestling with two ongoing issues that have defied resolution: the *crossover debate* over the present means by which CCM companies market their artists to the mainstream pop audience and the *lyric debate* concerning the role of the lyric in contemporary Christian music. The fact that we've continued to debate these issues is a good sign. Debate allows us time to learn from one another, challenge each other, and test our own understanding against true understanding—the voice of God revealed in the Scriptures.

Finally, there are the *voices of success* trumpeting ministry faithfulness and the recent achievements of CCM, telling of awards and honors, arenas filled to capacity, souls saved and lives changed, Christian artists at the top of the pop charts, unprecedented market share, and much more.

Caught as we are between the voices of criticism and the voices of success, its no wonder we have so many questions. Before we can get to the truth, we have to get our hearts and minds wrapped around the ideas that shape the Christian music community and the issues that concern it. By listening to the voices, we learn that the Christian music community is composed of wanted dissonance (unity in diversity), harmony (goodness, truth, and beauty), unwanted dissonance (strife and disunity), and unwanted harmony (choices that work to some degree but are either unnecessary or misapplied). As we listen to these voices, we must be prepared to rethink and reimagine our own image of Christian music.

"Not Enough Songs Mention Jesus Anymore"

In the spring of 1996, the board of directors from the WAY-FM Media Group placed a full-page ad in *CCM Magazine* titled "An Open Letter to the Christian Music Community."[2] The letter focused largely on the importance and historical precedent of using CCM as a tool for "winning young people to Jesus and discipling them in their walk."

"Not enough songs mention Jesus anymore," observed the writers of the letter. "Has the 'J' word all of the sudden become non-hip, or have we found that 'you' or 'he' has more power?"

"Yes...we believe there is a place to address social issues and love between two people occasionally. However, we hope that all of us involved in CCM will remember that our first priority is to be a lighthouse of truth in an ever increasing spiritual fog."

Live concerts gave WAY-FM reason for concern as well: "In our opinion, the gospel also has been diluted to some degree in live concerts. We have been disappointed in the last few years with some of the concerts our stations have promoted. In some instances, there has been little or no ministry throughout the entire event."

The letter closed with this request: "We are asking all of our friends in this 'industry,' and the body of Christ at large, to pray for the songwriters, artists, managers, producers, labels and radio stations. Pray that we will experience a fresh anointing and that the message in our music will clearly and creatively

...ry ...ustry insiders,

described, in MacLeod's words, "a vision that I received and the interpretation that unfolded regarding it." MacLeod published the vision hoping it would help those who "have been confused, disillusioned and wounded by the condition of what is now called the Christian music industry." According to MacLeod, "The vision was received while a small group of us were praying about this condition, and against the powers and principalities that have, and still do, control and manipulate much of what is called Christian music."[3]

The lobby in MacLeod's title refers to the lobby of the Nashville hotel and convention center where the annual Gospel Music Association convention is held each April. MacLeod recalls his vision: "The people were busy talking and going on with their business (what is commonly called schmoozing), each one dressed up in appropriate music attire, when much to my astonishment and horror I saw what looked like a massive snake lying on the lobby floor."[4] MacLeod described the lobby as "full of people who were busy 'lobbying' for position, power and their own agendas."[5]

The snake, MacLeod says, represents "the powerful evil spirits that plague and control much of the Christian music industry and much of Christendom."[6] The Snake Keepers are described as "the people who have been in power and have, knowingly or unknowingly, let the ways of the world enter into Christian music."[7]

"The Bottom Line"

In November 1997 Peoples Church of Salem, Oregon, announced its plans to terminate Jesus Northwest, the Christian music festival it had operated for twenty-one years. The announcement came in the form of a letter of repentance written by Peoples Church pastor and festival executive director Rev. Randy Campbell. Seeking forgiveness, Campbell wrote, "We humbly repent before the Lord and ask the forgiveness of the body of Christ for inadequately representing Christ in our ministry, message, and methods."

While the letter clearly expressed responsibility for specific sins for which Peoples Church claimed guilt, the letter also revealed that problems with CCM and others were contributing factors in the decision to terminate the festival: "Although the Lord is changing us, many problems still remain in the greater working of the contemporary Christian music industry, the Christian publishing industry, and independent ministries we have worked with over the years. These issues prevent us from being involved with the type of festival we've been providing. We feel that within these industries and ministries much of what is done (for example, ministry direction, decision-making methods, even the message itself) is often driven by marketing—not the mind of the Lord. It is driven by analyzing demographics, not His anointing, by audio/visual production, not His power or presence. Money, success and business have become the bottom line."[8]

"Reform and Return the Money"

On October 31, 1997, veteran CCM recording artist Steve Camp, describing himself as "burdened and broken over the current state of CCM," released an essay in poster form accompanied by 107 theses titled "A Call for Reformation in the Contemporary Christian Music Industry." Of all the voices of criticism, Camp's is arguably the most provocative. Along with studiously detailing CCM's shortcomings, Camp outlined specific steps he felt must be taken as well: "True revival is marked by repentance; true repentance brings

restitution; true restitution demands that Christian music be owned and operated only by believers whose aim is the glory of God consistent with Biblical
truth. *This means that the current CCMI (contemporary Christian music indus-*
try) labels must ~~~~ ~~~~ ~~~~

For instance, it is not unBiblical to consult non-Christian experts in
matters of business, craft or trade…but we can never engage in intimate binding—indissoluble relationships, alliances, or partnerships that
result in shared responsibility or authority for ministry purposes
(Deuteronomy 22:9-11; Philippians 2:14-15).[10]

On the subject of music itself, Camp, citing 1 Chronicles 16:37,42 takes a
definitive position: "Music, by Biblical definition, is a ministry." He concludes
his essay by urging the reader to "come away from an industry that has all but
abandoned Christ and forge, by God's grace, what it was always meant to be…a
ministry.… Pray on this, Pounding on Wittenberg's Door, let us come together
to make history—to make Contemporary Christian Music…Christian again."[11]

In November 2002 Steve Camp again addressed the Christian music
community with an open letter—this time in response to Chevrolet's spon-
sorship of the "Come Together and Worship Tour," featuring Michael W.
Smith, Third Day, and Max Lucado, and the charging of money to attend an
"evening of worship and evangelism." Camp explains in the letter that his
purpose is to "try to summarize those concerns as to why this event does not
function according to, nor is in practice consistent with the Scriptures; and,
therefore, cannot be honoring or glorifying to the Lord Jesus Christ."[12]

Debating the Lyric

On September 8, 1997, *CCM Update* published an article titled "Album Lyrics Raise Questions: Lack of 'Christian' content complicates Dove Award eligibility, chart placement decisions." The article brought out into the open a number of issues the CCM community had struggled with since Amy Grant's 1991 recording *Heart in Motion.* Chief among them was what makes one lyric "Christian" and another not, and when, if ever, the work of a Christian artist ceases to be categorized as "Christian." Predictably, Amy Grant received prominent mention, beginning with the lead paragraph "Amy Grant's new album *Behind the Eyes,* and others like it that don't necessarily reflect 'evangelical' lyric content, have spearheaded an industry discussion." The article also noted that the "Gospel Music Association (GMA) and Christian Music Trade Association (CMTA) have recently taken action to create new criteria and re-evaluate existing guidelines used to determine placement on sales charts and Dove Award eligibility."[13]

Sales-chart placement and Dove award eligibility are important and complex issues to many industry insiders, especially when mainstream artists are starting to find their way onto the CCM charts. Nevertheless, the issue for people like Rick Anderson, music buyer for Berean Christian Stores, is very simple: If there's no Christ, it's not Christian. Anderson appraised Grant's album *Behind the Eyes* by saying, "It's not a Christian album. A Christian album should be clear on the person of Christ and these lyrics are not."[14] The directness of his statement illustrates the intensity of the lyric debate: People have strong opinions about what makes something Christian, especially when it comes to lyrics. As a further example, consider that both the WAY-FM Network and the Air 1 Radio Network declined to play Grant's single "Takes a Little Time," citing a lack of "lyrical relevance" and failure to meet "lyrical criteria."

The GMA contacted a list of people "with diverse expertise and experience" in hopes of gathering various working definitions of *gospel music.*[15] Frank Breeden, former GMA president, told *CCM Update,* "I have no prediction for the outcome. It could be anything from 'we can't arrive at a definition' all the way to 'here it is.' "[16]

In July 1998 the GMA Board of Directors and the Dove Awards Com-mittee approved the following

and/or obviously prompted and informed by a Christian world view.[17]

Release of this definition unleashed a new round of criticisms and concerns. A sincere effort to resolve the question only added more fuel to the debate.

A Call for New Models

In 1999 Mark Joseph, a writer with a varied career in the entertainment busi-ness, published a book titled *The Rock & Roll Rebellion: Why People of Faith Abandoned Rock Music—and Why They're Coming Back.* In his book Joseph details the creation and development of what he refers to as the Christian music "ghetto" and describes the negative effect it has had on the culture at large. He claims that "the most damaging mistake made by leaders in the CCM industry over the years has been their dogged insistence on advancing contemporary Christian music as a separate genre of music."[18]

Joseph calls for change as he explains that "the faith community must acknowledge that the present system simply hasn't worked very well for taking their message out of the church and into the mainstream of American culture. It's time for that community to make music for the wider culture, as surely their leader would have done had he lived in the year 2000 and played a gui-tar. By doing this, they will not only lift the CCM culture out of inbred musi-cal stagnation, they will also bring life to a pop music world sorely in need of spiritual passion and creativity, something people who are in touch with the Creator of the universe presumably possess."[19]

A Flood of Success

This leads us to the other side of the discussion. While some voices are those of woe, warning, and regret, others celebrate CCM's financial success and growing popularity. Publicity and promotional muscle have secured Christian artists major national media exposure through the *Wall Street Journal,* National Public Radio, *Time, Newsweek, USA Today, LIVE with Regis and Kelly, Good Morning America, The Tonight Show with Jay Leno, The Late Show with David Letterman, ABC World News Tonight,* and others. Marketing to ancillary markets has also played an important role in CCM's success. For example, partnerships with record clubs Columbia House and BMG, and TV shopping programs such as QVC and the "Keep the Faith" infomercials have all proven profitable, increasing the consumer base of Christian music. Artists who have ties to the Christian music industry are regularly in *Billboard*'s chart of the top 200 albums each week.

While the issue of whether the music of Christian artists should cross over into the mainstream stirred much debate in the 1990s, for the most part these occurrences are now accepted and usually cause for celebration. In the Gospel Music Association's year-end report for 2003, president John Styll stated, "The second half of the year was historic in terms of crossover success. In the past, gospel music has gained general market prominence in one-shot situations, like God's Property's 'Stomp' and Bob Carlisle's 'Butterfly Kisses.' This year, we've had several artists, each with unique music styles, penetrate the mainstream in a significant way."[20] He went on to cite Stacie Orrico, MercyMe, Randy Travis, and Switchfoot as examples.

In a January 2004 interview with *The Tennessean,* a Nashville-based newspaper, EMI Christian Music Group CEO Bill Hearn explained it as a business strategy: "The core of our growth has to come from making great music and making music that appeals outside of the Christian subculture. We've been able to have some success with that in partnering with some of our EMI labels.

song "Change the World," recorded by Eric Clapton for the *Phenomenon* movie soundtrack. Through music licensing agreements and contracts for specific feature films, Christian artists have also written songs that have appeared in films such as *The Apostle, Dr. Dolittle, That Thing You Do! A Walk to Remember,* and *Bruce Almighty,* as well as on numerous television programs and even Super Bowl telecasts.

Live performances by Christian artists have had considerable impact as well. Christian concerts have become increasingly more professional and competitive with their mainstream counterparts. Artists like Michael W. Smith, Steven Curtis Chapman, and MercyMe regularly draw thousands of people a night to their concerts. NewSong's annual Winter Jam tour, which has been going on for nine years and includes a variety of CCM artists, had a record attendance of more than 115,000 people in 2004. A press release stated that "the 23-city tour saw over 5,000 attendees make the decision to follow Christ. In addition to receiving an overwhelming response to altar calls each night, the tour garnered nearly 2,500 sponsors for World Vision children."[22]

What's That Sound?

Many voices are eager to be heard in the CCM community, among them the voices of criticism, debate, and success. Though I could have given examples of many other voices, I chose these because I believe they are definitive in that the ideas they represent define the general ideological climate of CCM. These ideas, I believe, have influenced CCM from its beginning to the present. These are the ideas I want us to hear, transcribe, analyze, and test for truthfulness, quality, and kingdom perspective.

In 1981 I was a struggling twenty-four-year-old musician. I'd been married for six years and anesthetized with drugs and alcohol every single year. All my attempts at being a spiritual person were failures. Zen seduced me but could not hold me. Neither could the Tao. Transcendental meditation worked for a drummer friend of mine but not for me. Dianetics? Merely interesting science fiction. Krishnamurti held me for a moment, but only because Marc Johnson, the respected jazz bassist, had suggested him to me. Rudolph Steiner and anthroposophy turned out to be nothing more than a minor flirtation with something I couldn't even pronounce. And so it went.

At the beginning of my seventh year of marriage, I entered a recovery program where I was encouraged to believe that a power greater than I could restore me to sanity. Sanity, I came to realize, was the ability to think accurately and truthfully about the reality of life. I had not been thinking accurately or truthfully. I'd been following my feelings without checking them against the facts—against any sort of controlling narrative. The recovery program taught me a life-changing truth: Feelings aren't always facts. Feelings need to be checked against trustworthy stories. Somehow, in my first twenty-four years of life, I'd failed to develop a fact checker for my feelings and, as a result, ended up with an unreal life composed of too little truth—too few good, life-defining stories. This made it very difficult for me to live in the world.

Looking back over this strange and rocky period, I can point to the exact moment my sanity began to return. It was when I took what is known in recovery as a "fearless moral inventory." In a notebook I wrote an inventory of all the wrong I had done in my life (at least what I was conscious of at the time) and of all the people I had harmed in some way. It made me sick to my stomach. My life seemed to be an unbroken chain of miserably foolish choices, one after another, and I was reaping the full consequences of those choices. I read the notebook aloud to God and to a friend. God made no audible comment. The friend muttered, "That ain't nothin'." But he was wrong. It *was* something. It was convincing evidence that something was wrong in my life. I was humbled to find out that most of what was wrong began and ended with me. I had been thinking, speaking, living, and acting entirely for myself. It was time to repent, rethink, and reimagine life.

My notebook was instrumental in proving to me the biblical concept of sin. When I eventually heard the Jesus Story, I was undone because I understood myself to be a sinner in need of a Savior.

In similar fashion, throughout my career I have encountered all kinds of convincing evidence that CCM is made up of true, false, insufficient, and glorious ideas—some that ought to be wholeheartedly affirmed and others that demand immediate repentance. Yet this evidence will only be of real value to people who consider themselves sinners—or, in different language, those who realize they are capable of failure, of missing out on what it means to be truly human. Why? Because people who understand themselves to be sinful yet forgiven bearers of God's image are open to the possibility of having missed the mark in some way. *They are more afraid of not knowing the truth than of being found in error.* They regret naming anything false that is in reality true, or anything true that is in reality false. The really great sinners in the church and in the world are like that.

If we remain humble and contrite, we will in turn remain teachable, and God certainly delights in the teachable loser-sinner. If we want God in our midst—and I believe the CCM community does—we'll have to admit our sin and helplessness. The self-sufficient, as I know from past experience, have no need of God. When correction comes with grace (and it will—count on it), we will not regret it

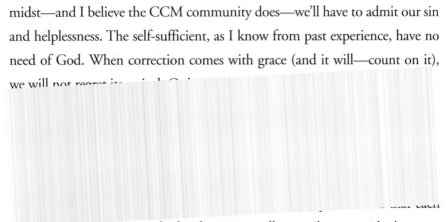

individual human error, whether large or small, contributes to what's wrong with the world. This principle applies to the world of CCM as well.

AMNESIACS TRAVELING THE SPIRITUAL MAP

I have a sense that many artists, industry people, and supporters of CCM are still traveling the spiritual map, searching for something more fantastic than the God of biblical Story, and yet all the while conducting their search in the name of the God that the Story alone describes. I also have a sense that our musical community is suffering from a prolonged attack of amnesia. It has caused us to forget that we're loser-sinners, and as a result we've thought too highly of ourselves. To forget that we're still people in need of a Savior is to forget how easily we can be fooled into feeling or thinking we're right about something, when in truth we are terribly wrong.

Our amnesia has also caused us to forget we're a people being renewed in the image of God, and consequently we've thought too lowly of ourselves. To forget this is to forget we're called to be God's direct representatives on earth, a distinctive people deeply and inextricably connected to their Creator and his purposes. We have no higher vocation than to be interested in the things that Jesus is interested in.

The beauty of the body of Christ is that when we do fall victim to amnesia, there are always a few fellow travelers still in possession of their kingdom memory. This is good news. It means there's always someone to show us the way home. If I lose my memory tomorrow, if I forget who I am in Messiah Jesus, I can count on someone to remind me. In this way the body of Christ is like the human body: Given the presence of spiritual truth and love, time and nurture, it will often heal itself. This gives me tremendous hope for the troubles that plague the CCM community. Healing begins with the truth, whether it be blood cells acting true to their function or the powerful truth of God's controlling Story. When brothers and sisters do become lost and forgetful, we serve them best by lovingly telling them the truth about their condition. No glossing over is needed; just the truth in love.

Christians do not—should not—surmise when it comes to living life. We're people in relentless pursuit of the new way to be human that Jesus modeled for us. And we're people who submit our ways of thinking to God's ways of thinking so they can be checked for untruths. Once we've considered the many voices in the CCM debate, once we've identified and extracted the core ideas, it's time to test those ideas against the new way Jesus taught and lived. We test them against this new way as best we understand it, and we also listen to the consensus of the saints in history. There is no other way. Our best guess, hunch, or feeling just will not do. All serious followers of Jesus, from the artists to the audience, should seek to bring the full and sufficient true Story to bear upon the subject of music, ministry, entertainment, and business.

We've much to gain from analyzing and testing the ideas contained within CCM. When we fail to build times of analysis and assessment (testing) into our lives, we fail to take up the tools of stewardship our Creator so purposefully created in us. Like our Creator, we're made to imagine, create, analyze, and assess. We possess these abilities because we bear God's image. The catch with being human and not God is that we're just as apt to imagine and create a mess as we are a masterpiece. Often we don't know what we have until we make time to stand back, analyze, and assess it.

In going through these steps, we're taking a close look at the imagination and ideology of a community, our community—artists, industry, and audience. First we test our choices to see if they're consistent with the voice of the Word. Then we ~~~~ ~~~~ ~~~~ ~~~~ ~~~~ ~~~~ ~~~~ ~~~~ ~~~~ ~~~~ ~~~~ in the process.

w no will I be today: a fool or a teachable sinner? Who will you be? Are we in pursuit of sufficient truth, and are we willing to apply it to our lives— including our creation, enjoyment, use, promotion, and sale of music? The shape and future of Christian music and its ability to contribute good and truth to the church and the world rest with our choices.

THE SOURCE OF THE TRUTH

Ironically, the Christian music community has existed without the full game plan of the Jesus way for too long. We've emphasized mission without any consensus or understanding as to what a true comprehensive mission for music might be in light of the kingdom of God. The mission will not be clear or unified unless, as J. I. Packer said, we live under the Word of God, "believing the teaching, trusting the promises, following the commands."

We begin with the understanding that everything created by God is very good. After creating, "God saw all that he had made, and it was very good" (Genesis 1:31). Our creational parents, Adam and Eve, perfectly reflected their Creator, mirroring his image faithfully. They were fully functioning creative beings in a perfect relationship of dependence upon God, thinking, speaking, and creating as his good, direct representatives. That is, until the Fall. The story of the Fall is the story of humanity's introduction to ideas that contradict the way to be human as revealed by God to his people. If Creation is the explanation for what's right with man and woman, the Fall clarifies what's wrong. The Creator gave the first living beings only one prohibition in his personal conversation with them, saying, "You must not eat from the tree of the knowledge of good and evil, for when you eat of it you will surely die" (Genesis 2:17). Along with his loving care, God gave man and woman one mystery: He purposely created a gap in their knowledge. It was up to man and woman to trust the Creator with the unknown, to let mystery be.

At the beginning of Genesis 3, the reader-hearer is introduced to a speaking creature called the serpent, who was "more crafty than any of the wild animals the LORD God had made. He said to the woman, 'Did God really say, "You must not eat from any tree in the garden"?' " (verse 1).

This challenge was the first volley of what would become an unprecedented battle between humans and Satan. Jesus would say of Satan, "He was a murderer from the beginning, not holding to the truth, for there is no truth in him. When he lies, he speaks his native language, for he is a liar and the father of lies" (John 8:44). The crafty serpent (inhabited by Satan) was testing the woman's knowledge of the Story. In effect, he was asking, "Do you actually know what God said?"

Since the beginning of Creation, the Creator has walked with his human creation in relationship, giving them all they need: provision and meaningful word and work. His care has been lovingly consistent and sustaining. He has faithfully spoken into human history and has graciously shown people a way of life that is right and good. He has shown men and women what it means to be interested in the same things he is interested in. What he's asked in return is that people trust his Word and live in light of it, with obedience and faithfulness. The first living beings failed to do this, and every generation since then has mistrusted God's Word.

Two thousand years ago God dealt a blow to the chronic mistrust by sending his Son Jesus to earth in the form of a man. Jesus came as the Word made flesh and stepped into the God-human story in an utterly unique way. He let people know that the time had arrived for something new: a kingdom way of being. God's old way of interacting with creation was over, and a new way had begun in Jesus. In this ~~~~~~~~~~~~

~~~~~~ (Romans 6.23). By grace through faith in Jesus, we've been saved from the penalty of sin. All followers of Jesus, including those who create, market, and enjoy CCM, have been called by God and equipped by the Holy Spirit to live as God's people, in God's place, under God's rule, right now, in these the in-between times. To live as God's people in God's place under God's rule is both a present and future kingdom mission and reality.

THE KINGDOM PERSPECTIVE

I'm highlighting the idea of a *comprehensive kingdom perspective* because I'm convinced that it will be of great help to the CCM community.[1] To gain a kingdom perspective is to get at reality. It is to see things as God sees them—that is, as much as any human can. It is to get the story straight—to have a sufficient and accurate picture of God acting in history on behalf of what he created. For pastor/author Scotty Smith, to see the kingdom "is to be overwhelmed with awe and joy at the enormity and glory of God's dominion."[2]

The kingdom is awesome and strangely subversive in that it subverts darkness, replacing it with light. It replaces old anti-Artist ways of being human with the new way of Jesus. Technically speaking, the kingdom is God's sovereign and saving reign and rule. His reign and rule is most evident when the interests of the King become the interests of the people, when individuals and communities faithfully live out what it means to follow Jesus. The kingdom is wherever and whenever the way of Jesus transforms people, place, and all ways of being, knowing, and doing.

A kingdom perspective is not a religious perspective. It is much bigger than that. A kingdom perspective informs us and teaches us that privatized ideas about salvation, such as accepting Jesus as your personal Savior, are so small that they cannot begin to do justice to the re-creation and transformation of humankind and creation that God has initiated in Christ. As Scotty Smith enthusiastically states, "Forgiveness is not the end; it's the beginning!"[3] In Adam we died, but in Christ we are made alive again, and "just as we have borne the likeness of the earthly man, so shall we bear the likeness of the man from heaven" (1 Corinthians 15:49). We are at the beginning again, for we "are being transformed into his likeness with ever-increasing glory, which comes from the Lord, who is the Spirit" (2 Corinthians 3:18). The new is here, and the old is passing away. The image of God in humankind is being renewed, and God's people are once again called to be in God's place under God's rule. This is the kingdom perspective that I believe the CCM community must come to embrace. And ultimately, there is no kingdom perspective apart from the Jesus way of being human. His storytelling and storied living point us in a kingdom direction. Our path is clear.

The Church

As significant as the church is to us, it should not be confused with the kingdom. Christians, who make up the church, are subjects in God's kingdom. The kingdom itself is something far more vast than the church. It is a huge reality composed of God's rule—his ways. Now, through Jesus, the rightness of God and relationship with him is accessible to everyone. Jesus stepped onto the stage of history as a historical fact of supreme and decisive importance, carrying with him other facts of supreme and decisive importance, and saying things such as, "I am the way and the truth and the life. No one comes to the

Father except through me" (John 14:6). Jesus clearly understood his purpose and the purpose of those he called as followers. He came to destroy death and bring life and immortality into the view of all people at all times so that every-one in every era would ~~...~~

~~...~~ The church is a community of people who believe this Story, who know through grace the object of true and ultimate worship—God the Father, God the Son, and God the Holy Spirit. Contrary to some notions, the church is not comprised of those who escape the real world to fuel up on an hour of worship in order to reenter real life. Instead, it consists of those who begin with the idea that true worship is real life, a life of doxology in which God is exalted, glorified, and proclaimed not only in the sanctuary but in every sphere of existence. The church is not meant to be a retreat from culture. Rather it has been called by God to shape culture by virtue of the church's distinctive-ness—its saltiness, its brightness.

Our day of worship is meant to frame and inform the intensity of our vision for the thinking, imagining, speaking, living, and creating we will do the rest of the week.

The Calling

Student-followers of Jesus are, as Os Guinness so succinctly puts it, called by him, to him, and for him.[4] This is our primary calling. We have returned to the kingdom pattern of Eden. We are God's people again, and as such we are called to live for him under his rule. We do his work, in his way, in his time.

We've been appointed by King Jesus to carry out a kingdom mission of bearing witness to him and to his kingdom ways. Guinness defines this mission as "everyone, everywhere, and in everything" thinking, speaking, living, and acting "entirely for him."[5] This kingdom mission is our secondary calling. Here again you can see a return to the kingdom pattern of Eden. We are called to be God's people in God's place, which is no longer the garden but is now defined as everywhere and in everything. God calls us to be salt and light in every sphere of existence from the church to the boardroom. These two concepts: God's people, in God's place, under God's rule and everyone, everywhere, and in everything accurately reflect a comprehensive kingdom perspective of calling and mission.

If the CCM community is composed of Christians who desire to live in response to God's calling, then we must see ourselves as subjects in God's kingdom. We must see ourselves as one among many communities of Christian enterprise, thinking, speaking, living, and acting entirely for Jesus. The CCM community is not just a group of individuals who listen to contemporary Christian music, who earn money from it in some way, and who claim to have a personal relationship with Messiah Jesus. This is far too weak a description. Like the church, the CCM community is made up of people whom God has chosen and grafted together as a new humanity. They are a part of the body of Christ of which Christ is the head. The members of the body of Christ are dependent on Jesus and on one another.

Before we can hope to tell good and true stories through music, which is our secondary calling, we must first acknowledge and live in light of our primary calling as followers of Jesus. Everything else in our lives is meant to be lived out in response to this central truth. The truth that Christians have a primary calling by God, to God, and for God is the starting place for thinking about all secondary callings, including Christian music.

Secondary Callings

God has given us meaningful secondary callings through which we can use our imaginations, express our creativity, and mirror his holiness. Here, calling is connected to the biblical idea of dominion or ruling. Like God, whose eternal kingdom is his reign, realm, authority, ways, and dominion, humankind has been given dominion over the earth. Dominion, introduced in Genesis 1:26-27 should

... governors over creation. As with any high office, accountability and responsibility come with the position. Humans are accountable to the Sovereign for the way they govern. God has equipped us to rule with love and wisdom, and we are not permitted to exploit creation for selfish purposes. To be anything but careful with what God has made is to mishandle his creativity. To mishandle his creativity is to misunderstand the seriousness of our role as his representatives on earth. Everything that has and will continue to develop out of this stewardship role must be seen in light of our primary calling. Everywhere we go and in everything we do, we should purpose to live by the truth that we are called by him, to him, and for him. We are not called by ourselves, to ourselves, or for ourselves. This describes the old way of self-perspective, not the new way of kingdom perspective.

Consider Psalm 90 as an example of our secondary calling being intertwined with our primary calling:

> And let the beauty of the LORD our God be upon us,
>   And establish the work of our hands for us;
> Yes, establish the work of our hands. (verse 17, NKJV)

We are first called to God, to his presence. The psalmist is asking that the presence of God be upon the people of God. He is asking for something of

God's quality and character to begin the work, to establish it, to be its starting place. The psalmist understands that it is God who inspires the work of the hands that serve him, and it is God who has the power to give the work eternal significance.

When we place all of our thinking, speaking, and doing under the banner of calling, all of life is infused with true meaning and purpose. Life becomes something far bigger than our own personal happiness and survival. A kingdom calling also inspires an integrated life and works against the disease of dualism and compartmentalization. The banner of kingdom calling is huge. It includes, says Ken Meyers, "not just a person's occupation from 9 to 5, but also his or her role as a spouse, parent, citizen, and neighbor—in short, the whole of one's identity under God."[6]

The importance of a person's calling is not determined by whether it resembles occupations that are often categorized as "full-time Christian service." As Elton Trueblood wisely pointed out years ago, "It is a gross error to suppose that the Christian cause goes forth solely or chiefly on weekends."[7] In reality, all followers of Jesus are in full-time Christian service. Unfortunately, a few callings, primarily those of pastors and missionaries (and musicians), have defined this phrase for us and, as a result, the impact of God's people everywhere and in everything has been limited. This has in turn led to confusion over the idea of ministry. The church in general, and the people of CCM specifically, must commit to restoring the idea that all secondary callings are important and that everyone has the potential to serve and tell trustworthy stories. We cannot afford to relax our grip on this truth. To do so is to invite a double-life view in which callings are divided into the sacred and the secular. The danger with this kind of dualism, says Os Guinness, is that it narrows "the sphere of calling." Instead of everyone, everywhere, and in everything, you quickly end up with a few people, in a few places, doing a few things entirely for God.

DIVERSITY AND FAITHFULNESS

Any teaching that narrows the scope and sphere of calling by promoting cer-

Dan Haseltine of Jars of Clay believes his band's role in this vast calling (as it pertains to music and lyric) is to "prepare people to hear the Word of God, to start [them] down the path of thinking about eternal things."[8] The members of Jars of Clay do not, however, advocate this for everyone and are in full support of musicians who directly proclaim the gospel from the stage. Charlie Lowell, keyboardist for the band, puts it this way: "Some seem to have a view of the body of Christ as this head and twenty-eight arms. We see it as different kinds of people with various gifts, doing different services, having different careers, and using their specific gifts differently. We wish the church would be open to this and encouraging of it, instead of questioning it or trying to redefine it."[9] One Christian who isn't trying to redefine the body of Christ is Trevor McNevan of Thousand Foot Krutch, who says, "There are a lot of awesome Christian bands doing an amazing job who are called to minister to kids in the church. But from day one I've always felt drawn to those outside of the church—I have a heart for the cry of those kids. That's really where we feel led."[10]

Our mission should be to faithfully answer to our own calling and not tear down the callings of others. In this way Jars of Clay and Thousand Foot Krutch have modeled for us a kingdom perspective. Faithfulness to individual callings while keeping our primary calling in focus—being student-followers of Jesus—is the starting place for cultivating a comprehensive kingdom perspective of music.

Let me also add that faithfulness to one's calling is ultimately the only true measure of success. By your faithfulness you will change people and creation according to God's plan. Write these words on your heart:

> Do not throw away your confidence; it will be richly rewarded. You need to persevere so that when you have done the will of God, you will receive what he has promised. For in just a very little while,

> "He who is coming will come and will not delay.
>   But my righteous one will live by faith.
> And if he shrinks back,
>   I will not be pleased with him."

> But we are not of those who shrink back and are destroyed, but of those who believe and are saved. (Hebrews 10:35-39)

One reason for respecting a life lived by faith is the freedom that comes with not having to have every choice you make produce an immediate tangible result. The result may not even be seen in your lifetime. Faith in God and his will for our lives frees us from faith in man and the lie of pragmatism. Oh, how our community needs this! Oh, how I need it. Instead of living as people pleasers, we can live for God in response to his grace and love. Instead of living under the lie of pragmatism, thinking that whatever works must be good, we can be a people set free to start at good. Then whether good choices cause us to fail or to succeed by the world's standards is of no importance.

May God give us present and future grace to live as his called people, everywhere and in everything, under the banner of his kingdom and to his glory.

SIN AT THE CROSSROADS

How do we begin to understand accusations of sin in the CCM camp? At this

industry, that "non-Christian" music is at the top of the CCM charts, that
Christian music is at the top of the pop charts, that money and success have
become the bottom line, or whatever the problem might be, one thing remains
absolutely constant: the truth of God's Word and its timeless ability to suffi-
ciently explain our past, present, and future struggles.

The book of Hebrews speaks of our struggle against sin (see Hebrews 12).
The book of Galatians tells us that "the Scripture declares that the whole world
is a prisoner of sin" (3:22), and Romans reminds us that "there is no one right-
eous, not even one" (3:10). And in case we've forgotten, there is 1 John 1:8,
"If we claim to be without sin, we deceive ourselves and the truth is not in us."

Concurrent with the reality of sin, we can also be assured that God is committed to changing every human being who has trusted in Jesus for the forgiveness of his or her sin. Amazingly enough, he's changing people whom I
don't like and with whom I disagree! It's important to remember that the new
kingdom opportunity is an ongoing process. It is true that Christians cooper-
ate with the process, but nevertheless they remain God-dependent throughout
the process.

Sin problems will exist in CCM as long as there are people in CCM. This
admission should not be construed as a license to sin. It is an acceptance of
our present kingdom reality—not the kingdom coming, but the kingdom at
hand. Is anyone really surprised that sin, error, misplaced priorities, confusion,

and disunity can be found in CCM? If we're to be surprised about anything, it ought to be that there is still grace for people with such short memories.

Speaking the Truth in Love

Are we to "put off falsehood" and speak the truth to one another in love (see Ephesians 4:15,25)? Are we to speak "only what is helpful for building others up according to their needs, that it may benefit those who listen" (verse 29)? Are we to rid ourselves of "all bitterness, rage and anger, brawling and slander, along with every form of malice" (verse 31)? Yes, yes, yes. But this is difficult stuff. It's hard to tell a brother or sister in Christ that he or she is in error. And it's hard to accept someone pointing out our own transgressions. Well, relationship is messy. For that matter, the kingdom life at hand is extremely messy.

But Christians are not spiritual free agents. We are called by God, to God, and for God. For this reason we must take accusations of spiritual unfaithfulness and visions of partnering with the devil very seriously. And we must take accusations of having sinned against brothers and sisters as serious cause for self-examination and repentance.

None of us can afford to blow off our critics. We cannot avoid entering the debates or speaking the truth in love. And we don't dare become too impressed with ourselves and our symbols of success. All accusations of sin, conflicts, criticisms, and debates ought to cause us to cry out to God, begging him to examine our motives and expose our self-deception. This is not to say, however, that ideas shouldn't be debated, prophecies tested, or accusations challenged. Don't be afraid to hear the sound of your voice answering these accusing voices. Part of taking these voices seriously is debating, testing, and challenging them when necessary. It also means treating any person—especially a fellow believer who takes issue with you personally or with CCM in general—with the dignity and respect due to a fellow image-bearer of God. Pray to speak or write in such a way that love for God, his truth, and his church outweighs self-interest and wrong motives. Mocking, despising, and ridiculing others are not actions that reflect Christ. Reject them.

It is my belief that the Christian music community must come to under stand that

...orth living: being God's man or woman in God's place under God's rule. It is to live for God everywhere and in everything. There are no small roles in this story. We cannot and must not put borders around it. The question is, Will we, the artists, the industry, and the audience of CCM, enter into the Story with faith and imagination, with sufficient reverence and awe? Fifteen years ago my friend Margaret Becker sang these simple but essential words: "I commit." And so must everyone who takes seriously Jesus's new way to be human.

...ᴜ or the Sadducees two thousand years ago, "You are in error because you do not know the Scriptures or the power of God" (Matthew 22:29). The same can often be said of those of us who labor in Christian music, as well as of those who buy it, listen to it, and champion it. We can trace the reasons for our error to the earliest stirrings of the CCM industry.

Contemporary Christian music was born of the Jesus movement of the late '60s and early '70s and was, in fact, originally known as "Jesus music." This revival among young people was by most accounts a tremendous sovereign work of God, a unique time when God called out his children from among the massive tribe of youth, ranging from suburban young people to disenfranchised hippies. In a 1972 article in *U.S. News & World Report,* Billy Graham declared it "by and large a genuine movement of the Spirit of God."[1]

Reflecting on the "street" element of the Jesus movement, social critic Ken Myers wrote, "The Jesus People were essentially Christian hippies, an unorganized assortment of relatively new believers who were adamant in their eagerness to construct their fellowship and worship according to the sensibility of the counterculture."[2]

U.S. News & World Report further expanded on this idea:

Many Jesus people—or Jesus freaks as they sometimes call themselves—once belonged to the youth revolt and a counterculture aimed at tearing down adult values. Today, they are emerging, disillusioned, from that experience. But they retain from the revolt's credo a passion for experience, not rationalism. Their biggest meetings often are held in large churches that offer them hospitality—but their suspicion of institutions extends to the institutional church.[3]

There was indeed a strong suspicion of institutions among many of the new converts. They sincerely believed God was working in a new way through the Jesus movement and, consequently, was not about to pour new wine into old wineskins. In this climate, nondenominational fellowships flourished. These fellowships had a look and sound unlike any of the mainline denominations, or any Christian fellowship before them. Many of the young people who came to Christ during the Jesus movement eventually found their way back to mainline denominational fellowships, yet many more helped establish the new, largely charismatic, nondenominational fellowships, including communes modeled after the lives of Christians described in the book of Acts (2:44). The well-known and respected Jesus People USA commune is still thriving today in downtown Chicago, though it is now affiliated with a denomination.

More than anything, the Jesus movement focused on these four elements:

1. The imminent return of Jesus in the form of the Rapture
2. The worship of God using contemporary instrumentation and style
3. Evangelism and the use of music in evangelism, especially evangelism targeted at youth
4. Charismatic renewal

Within the nondenominational fellowships, two influential theological positions took root: (1) a renewed dependence on the Holy Spirit and an emphasis on his work as well as the manifestation of the gifts of the Spirit, and

(2) an eschatology (view of the end times) emphasizing the pretribulation rapture of the church. The idea of the church being raptured or suddenly taken
out of the world by Christ is based upon 1 Thessalonians 4:16-17.[4]

synergistic pair. Thus, the theological ideas common to the Jesus and charismatic movements were common to CCM's beginnings as well.

Though the charismatic movement's renewed emphasis on the Spirit's role
in the believer's life was positive in many ways, this emphasis had its downside.
By emphasizing the work and gifts of the Holy Spirit, especially spontaneous
revelational prophesying and speaking in tongues, the focus shifted from
knowing God through his revealed Story to knowing God through experience.
This in turn shifted the focus from thinking to feeling, wherein for many
believers, their experience became as much the measure of truth as the sure
Word of Truth. Subjective, private experiences—hunches, spontaneous prophecies, intuitions, visions, and hearing God speak inside one's head—were often
given equal authority with Scripture—and in some cases more. For some
Christians, the desire for charismatic experiences gradually eclipsed their desire
to learn of God through the Bible. Charismatic experience came to be perceived as a more personal, tangible, and valuable encounter with God than
the encounter that comes by reading and meditating over the Spirit-inspired
Word of God. The fallout from this view of life in the Spirit was substantial.
When anything like a Christian world-and-life view was articulated in the
public arena, it was likely to be in the form of a severely truncated witness,
such as, "Hey, man. Do you know Jesus Christ as your personal Savior?"

People might have been bold enough to ask the question, but few were bold enough, or adequately equipped, to witness to the authority and influence of Jesus over every sphere of life. While evangelism brought people into the church, biblically informed ways of thinking and doing were seldom brought to bear upon the ideas driving culture outside the walls of the sanctuary. Very few Christians understood the necessity of cultivating a comprehensive theology.

Shaky Ground

This emphasis on experience contributed to an already existing suspicion of and disrespect for the word *theology* itself, especially as it might relate to education received at seminary. For many, theology meant dead orthodoxy, and a seminary education was largely considered to be useless. The depth of distrust of academic study among many of CCM's pioneers is probably best characterized by Keith Green's reference to seminary as something more akin to a *cemetery*.[5]

Green's remark, though flippant, accurately reflected the suspicion that words like *seminary* and *theology* inspired. While Bible studies were viewed by most as essential for God to speak into the believer's life, many charismatics were taught, directly and through the modeling of leaders and other believers, that God was eager to speak to them through the still, small voice inside their heads, through tongues and interpretation, and through the prophesies of church leaders.

Seminary training was considered unnecessary for the most part. However, Pastor Chuck Smith of Calvary Chapel in Costa Mesa, California—a charismatic and a gifted Bible expositor—has boldly admitted that "one of the greatest weaknesses of the charismatic movement is its lack of sound Bible teaching."[6] This is not an affordable weakness. Neither is it a weakness common only to charismatic brethren.

The charismatic movement's emphasis on the Holy Spirit and experience is not by itself the issue. It's important to note that the movement's emphasis on the important work of the Holy Spirit has helped remind millions of believers of the Spirit's role in the Christian life. The difficulty comes with our human propensity to emphasize one imp̶o̶r̶t̶a̶n̶t̶ ̶i̶d̶

... come up snort because we have not adequately studied God's Word and applied it to the whole of life. This has contributed to our lack of biblically comprehensive theologies for the enjoyment and use of music, and for faithfully interacting with the business of music.

If the fullness of God's revealed truth in the Bible is not taught and applied to the fullness of life, if our experiences and our God-thoughts are not interpreted and corrected by God's own thoughts, then it is certain our ways of thinking and doing will be insufficient to speak to life's challenges, especially to the challenge of engaging with culture. Our faith journey must be founded on the controlling narrative of God's Word to us. If it is not, we will inevitably stray from the path of faithfulness to Jesus and the mission and kingdom perspective he has given us.

Continue in What You Have Learned

I'm aware that I'm using Scripture here to make the point that Scripture is important, but I think we can learn from Paul's reminder to Timothy:

> But as for you, continue in what you have learned and have become
> convinced of, because you know those from whom you learned it,
> and how from infancy you have known the holy Scriptures, which
> are able to make you wise for salvation through faith in Christ Jesus.

All Scripture is God-breathed and is useful for teaching, rebuking, correcting and training in righteousness, so that the man of God may be thoroughly equipped for every good work. (2 Timothy 3:14-17)

With regard to prophecy, Peter explains,

Above all, you must understand that no prophecy of Scripture came about by the prophet's own interpretation. For prophecy never had its origin in the will of man, but men spoke from God as they were carried along by the Holy Spirit. (2 Peter 1:20-21)

What many contemporary believers who prophesy words of foretelling or prediction often miss is that the Bible also speaks of prophesying as proclaiming or declaring truth. Contrary to popular ideas, the prophets of old prophesied not as much in the role of foretelling as in the role of proclaiming what God had personally taught and instructed them to proclaim. New-covenant believers have this same role with regard to Scripture. To proclaim Scripture is to prophesy. In other words, a high view of prophecy and a high view of Scripture are not mutually exclusive positions. In Malachi 4:5 the prophet foretold the coming of John the Baptist. In Acts 2:1-38 we have the record of Peter, filled with the Holy Spirit, proclaiming the Scriptures with power. To prophesy is to declare truth under the guidance of the Spirit, whether it is by predicting, foretelling, or some other means.

Even so, we often invest in extraordinary experiences rather than in the extraordinary study and speaking of God's Word. I think it is fair to say that the other-worldliness of spiritual gifts is one of the things that make them attractive to us. Many of them seem to exist in a state beyond rational verification, which contributes to a sense of comfort—they're so out of the ordinary, they must be from God. When we experience God in this way, we often feel as if we've been removed from the humdrum of normal life and brought a little closer to heaven. We feel as if we've been lifted out of this world into the presence of God. He might speak to us like an intimate friend or lay us out flat on our backs. The unpredictability is both frightening and exciting.

If this is in fact a worthy and accurate

more specifically, they do not replace the word-and-work model of Jesus, that of storytelling and storied living after his own pattern of being human in the world.

Engaging in the study of God's controlling narrative for life will not prevent me from experiencing charismata or revival, nor will it in any way diminish my high view of the present work of the Holy Spirit. On the contrary, it prepares me to carry out the very human role assigned to me by the defining nature of the spiritual gifts God has given me. In reality, every true follower of Messiah Jesus is a charismatic, for the Scripture makes plain that "the manifestation of the Spirit is given to each one for the profit of all" (1 Corinthians 12:7, NKJV).

Only the Word and the Spirit working together will adequately equip us to test all things, hold on to the good, and abstain from evil. Nothing else will do, no matter how convincing it appears at first. All our thinking and doing, whether or not we believe it to be Spirit-inspired, must be tested by our present understanding of the Word and, when necessary, corrected by it. Without the starting place of God's Word, the Christian life would be a subjective free-for-all composed of far too little truth to be of any significance. The same applies to Christian music.

Am I saying that God does not guide his people by the Spirit with feelings and impressions of his will? Absolutely not. However, just because God can guide his people in any way he chooses does not mean that his people should abandon careful study of his Spirit-inspired Word. Regardless of whether we call ourselves cessationists, charismatics, Pentecostals, or advocates of the third wave, none of us can afford to carve away at the authority and necessity of Scripture by equating those who hear from God via spontaneous revelation as being deeply connected to the agenda of God, while saying that men and women who read, meditate on, and pray the Scriptures are not. This kind of thinking does not serve to build up the church or tell a good story to those outside the church who watch and critique. It certainly does not help the Christian music community equip itself with the knowledge necessary to faithfully engage with both the church and the culture at large.

THE JESUS MOVEMENT TODAY

In spite of the good that came from an emphasis on the work and gifts of the Spirit during the Jesus and charismatic movements, CCM became the product of an environment where it was not only acceptable to de-emphasize learning of God from his Word, but such foolishness was (and still is) sometimes encouraged. Without the Story, we are left to take our best guesses on how to proceed with artistry, ministry, and commerce. And our best guesses are far from the best. How can those in the CCM community possibly choose to continue in this way, allow themselves to be influenced in this way, or support this kind of thinking when to do so is to willfully ignore God's thoughts and God's words? This is the crossroads.

The writings of eighteenth-century theologian Jonathan Edwards have been a great help to me in shaping what I hope is a charitable and balanced view of the role of Scripture, the Holy Spirit, and the Spirit's gifts in the Christian life. In his treatise *Distinguishing Marks of a Work of the Spirit of God,* Edwards wrote:

My design therefore at this time is to show what are the true, certain, and distinguishing evidences of a work of the Spirit of God, by which we may safely proceed in judging of any operation we find in ourselves, or see in others.

Having established that the Scriptures are our only trustworthy guide, Edwards also observed:

> The Holy Spirit is sovereign in his operation; and we know that he uses a great variety; and we cannot tell how great a variety he may use, within the compass of the rules he himself has fixed. We ought not to limit God where he has not limited himself.[8]

From here Edwards stated that in his experience of revival and dramatic manifestations of the Spirit, there are certain kinds of behavior and imaginings that are neither evidence for, nor evidence against, a work being of the Spirit of God. These kinds of behavior and imaginings range from the extraordinary way in which minds are affected to the extraordinary effects on the bodies of people "such as tears, trembling, groans, loud outcries, agonies of body, or the failing of bodily strength."[9]

According to Edwards,

> We cannot conclude that persons are under the influence of the true Spirit because we see such effects upon their bodies, because this is not given as a mark of the true Spirit; nor on the other hand, have we any

reason to conclude, from such outward appearances, that persons are not under the influence of the Spirit of God, because there is no rule of Scripture given us to judge of spirits by, that does either expressly or indirectly exclude such effects on the body, nor does reason exclude them.[10]

Everyone in CCM must give honest consideration to where they stand on their view of Scripture and their view of the work of the Holy Spirit.[11] Put aside for a moment such labels as "charismatic" and "noncharismatic," "anointed" and "not anointed," "revivalists" and "dead churches." Take a vacation from your socialized surroundings and go to God's Word. Find out *why* you believe the way you do. Have you framed your Christian life by what the Bible says, or are your choices enculturated responses to your present worship environment? If you are in an environment that emphasizes the Word but seldom speaks of the Spirit's role and power, would this explain your inclination to speak and act with the same emphasis? Likewise, if you are in an environment that emphasizes the gifts of the Spirit and learning of God through subjective experiences, could this explain why you tend to embrace similar views? We are called to worship God in spirit and in truth. Both are necessary for acceptable worship.

I came to a knowledge of the Jesus Story through the preaching of the Word—a telling of the good news after the pattern of Jesus. So naturally I'm inclined to acknowledge the Scriptures as God-breathed words of eternal life. I'm inclined to see them as instruction and correction. Should I now abandon the very words that the Spirit used to bring me life? I sometimes wonder if many of us aren't looking for something other than "training in righteousness" (2 Timothy 3:16). How about you? Are you looking for something other than being "thoroughly equipped for every good work" (verse 17)? For that matter, have any of us finished our training, completed every good work, and now become so bored with life that we're twiddling our thumbs as we await instructions from on high? Absolutely not! We are not through with the clearly revealed Story because God is not through with us. He is still using it to train and equip people for the Jesus way, for the kingdom life.

...study and for-
...mation or a comprehensive biblical framework for CCM, as well as the calling to care for creation, to a very low point on the list of priorities. As a result, few Christians gave much thought to Jesus's admonition to be salt in the world—to be as my friend, author Bob Briner, said, a Roaring Lamb. And with good reason. It's difficult to be a Roaring Lamb, concerned with living for God everywhere and in everything, when you are preoccupied with being caught up with Jesus in the clouds.

The Rapture (a term that does not explicitly appear in Scripture) is a premillennialist doctrine especially common to the people of the Jesus movement, to the nondenominational churches of the era, and to charismatics in particular. It is a doctrine that refers to the church being caught up in the clouds with the Lord at his Second Coming (see 1 Thessalonians 4:15-18). Premillennialists in general are divided over when the Rapture will occur. Some say before the great tribulation, others midway through, still others believe it will occur after the tribulation period. The view most common to CCM's Jesus movement/charismatic movement roots is the first view, known as pretribulationism or "pretrib" for short. The pretrib view divides the Second Coming of the Lord into two stages. First, Jesus will come for his church before the Great Tribulation via the Rapture. During the tribulation the saints will remain with Jesus. Following the tribulation victory, the church will appear with Jesus at his Second Coming (which under this scenario would actually be a third coming).

According to the *Dictionary of Christianity in America,* "This view gained ascendancy in American premillennial circles before World War I, thanks in large part to *The Scofield Reference Bible,* and (later in the 1970s) with…Hal Lindsey's best-selling *The Late Great Planet Earth.*"[12]

One cannot underestimate the influence Scofield and Lindsey had on the Jesus movement, the charismatic renewal movement, and on CCM's earliest beginnings. The key to understanding their effect on CCM lies in one very important assertion common to both: that all prophetic events previously impeding the return of Christ have been fulfilled and that Christ's coming for his church is imminent. CCM veteran John Fischer underscores the effect and consequences of this idea on contemporary Christian music:

> One thing that's important I think in grabbing the mood of those early days was that there was really absolutely no thinking of careers. That was not in our minds. At least it certainly wasn't in mine. There was this idea that you were on the edge of the world, and you're not thinking about tomorrow. You're thinking about now, and the only thing we knew about tomorrow was the Lord's coming back. And sing it now, and get the word out now, and change the world now, and we don't have much time. That's exactly what we all thought.[13]

While the focus on the imminent Rapture seemed to create the feeling of being absolutely sold out to Jesus and ready for his summons, history has proved that faithfulness and readiness are not as conveniently predictable or as easily defined as CCM's pioneers once thought. Fischer commented on this as well: "What happened with the late '70s was kind of slowly creeping in the idea that, *Wait a minute, we do have the rest of our lives here.*"[14]

CCM's originators learned what Christians throughout the ages have discovered: No person can know the day or the hour of Christ's coming (see Matthew 24:36,42). We are to be prepared for his coming, but in no way should a by-product of this preparedness be a failure to equip ourselves for and carry out cultural engagement. CCM's pioneers made this exact error and, as a result, were left without directions on how to proceed with the future. The idea of becoming

not just a message of personal salvation but the whole wonderful Story of redemption from Genesis to Revelation. Not only must we know it, but we must prayerfully seek Spirit-wisdom to apply it in our daily lives. By learning the whole of Scripture, we are able to construct truthful, sufficient theologies of everything necessary to life, from culture and music to parenting and business. In this way, whether at home or in Nepal, at church or in the workplace, the story we live, the story we speak, and the story we sing will by its truthfulness and authenticity be attractive to those who do not follow the Jesus way.

The preparation necessary to live and share the Jesus Story is far more complex than the preparation necessary to meet Jesus in the clouds. In the latter, I must know Jesus and be known by him in order to be included in his Second Coming. In the former, I must know Jesus, be known by him, and be learning of him from his Word. In the time I'm given, I must learn and study the Scriptures in order to accurately bring the Word of Truth to bear upon all of life—in everything from human sexuality, capitalism, and child-rearing to music and retail merchandising. Until Jesus summons his church, I should do nothing but live the good life—a life so good, so imaginative, so thought-provoking, so truthful, so compelling that it shouts to the world, "Hey, world! The good Story is alive in me!"

Having become convinced that this lifetime would indeed be cut short by the Rapture, many of CCM's pioneers failed to develop a comprehensive biblical framework for CCM artistry, industry, and audience. Zealous for Jesus's return, they thought it necessary only to prepare themselves and others for the afterlife. Armed with this conviction, many of these brothers and sisters believed that the primary purpose of contemporary Christian music was to take the message of salvation to young people. They quickly discovered they were not alone, finding sympathetic support from an unlikely place—the Recreation Department of the Baptist Sunday School Board, now LifeWay Christian Resources of the Southern Baptist Convention.

The Southern Baptists, like their Jesus movement and charismatic movement brethren, came to recognize that contemporary rock and pop music could speak to young people in powerful ways. While the largely nondenominational charismatics were busy using music to fill churches (such as Calvary Chapel) with new young believers, the Baptist mission began to use music both to evangelize and to keep Baptist youth interested and involved in the Baptist church. The idea of introducing contemporary music to Baptist youth was not a collective decision on the part of the Southern Baptist Convention. It was, however, given birth under their roof by a handful of Baptists led by a young music minister named Billy Ray Hearn. It all started with the creation of the first Christian folk musical *Good News*.

SOMETHING FOR THE KIDS

In the summer of 1997, thirty years after *Good News* was first produced, I revisited this historic event with three of the men who made it happen—Billy Ray Hearn, Ralph Carmichael, and Elwyn Raymer.[1] Hearn recalled how *Good News* got its start:

> When *Good News* was created, I was a minister of music at the First Baptist Church in Thomasville, Georgia. The Recreation Department of the Baptist Sunday School Board was interested in bringing music into their recreation programs for youth, and I was the guy who knew about that stuff and could do fun music for the kids. So they asked me to come speak about how I thought I could incorporate music for youth into their recreation programs. This was during the time when churches were building gymnasiums and trying to show that the church could meet a lot of the needs of families, including recreation. The music they wanted me to do wasn't supposed to be church music; the church already had its own music. This was supposed to be music for outside the church.

I asked Hearn why they settled on the idea of a youth musical and not something in keeping with the pop music of the time, such as the Rolling Stones or the Beatles. Hearn replied,

> About this same time, along came this group called Up With People that did a youth musical kind of thing. They were emphasizing God and country. I saw that and the reception it was getting and thought, *Do what Up With People does, but only with more gospel in it.* So it was

really through the Recreation Department that youth-oriented music made its way into the Baptist churches, starting with a musical we developed at Ridgecrest and Glorieta called *Good News*.

..........,   ᴇlwyn ʀaymer from the Baptist Sunday School Board came to Glorieta to write it down and put it in a form that could be sent out to the churches so they could perform it."

Raymer remembers being none too happy about his assignment: "I worked for the Church Music Department, and this was coming out of the Department of Recreation, so I came to it a little snobbish."

Snobbish or not at the outset, Raymer recalls his change of heart: "It was my job as a music editor for the Sunday School Board to get the music for *Good News* into print and onto disc. We took some equipment down to a big youth-music gathering at Glorieta over Christmas and stayed up all night recording it in a rough fashion. *Good News* changed my life, because I had to face that God had his hand on it, and that I was wrong about it."

Good News was hugely successful, with the Sunday School Board selling about 300,000 copies. Raymer notes,

> The Baptists as a denomination did have a great organization in order to disseminate things. So once something was noticed as good and worthwhile, it could be disseminated throughout thousands of churches.

This was just the beginning. The Recreation Department of the Baptist Sunday School Board had sparked something big. Hearn tells it this way:

People really started getting excited about this kind of thing when I brought 1,300 vocalists and 50 orchestra members, all kids, to do *Good News* at the Southern Baptist Convention that year in Houston. We performed right before Billy Graham spoke. Some of the Word Records people were there and said afterwards, "We gotta do this kind of thing." Later, Word wanted to know if I would leave the church work I was doing to come to their headquarters in Waco, Texas. I was hired as their director of music promotion and right away started developing another musical with Ralph Carmichael and Kurt Kaiser.

Kurt Kaiser, a composer employed by Word Records, flew in to attend the Houston event and meet with Hearn. With enthusiasm high, Kaiser and Hearn decided to phone Ralph Carmichael, a respected composer/arranger for Bing Crosby, Peggy Lee, and Nat King Cole, to discuss the possibility of creating more youth-oriented musicals for the church.

Carmichael, a friend of Kaiser's and already a partner with Word through his own Light Records, recalls the telephone conversation: "One night I got a call from Billy Ray Hearn about doing something for the kids. He wanted to see if I'd be interested in experimenting, with doing some things musically to see if we couldn't get the kids interested. Out of that came *Tell It Like It Is*."

Carmichael remembers, "We wanted the ring of honesty, cutting through the churchy vernacular. We first recorded it with The Baylor Religious Hour Choir at a studio in Dallas.... My dream was to give the kids their own music."

THE MUSICAL/CULTURAL GAP

Some readers will have begun to suspect a gap between the music kids were listening to on pop radio, or on *The Ed Sullivan Show*, and the music these three men had in mind. In 1967–68 a handful of the artists and songs popular with "the kids" were: "Ruby Tuesday" by The Rolling Stones, "Light My Fire" by

The Doors, "Hey Jude" by The Beatles, and "Mrs. Robinson" by Simon and Garfunkel.[2] Of these, only Simon and Garfunkel were even remotely close to what these men had created or were intent on creating.

There are at least two good r...

...ond reason, and probably the more important one, is the context. You cannot understand the musical gap between *Good News* and "Hey Jude" unless you have some sense of the context and setting of the denominational church in 1967–68. What Christian groups like Third Day, Relient K, and Pillar take for granted today, men like Ralph Carmichael, Billy Ray Hearn, and Kurt Kaiser fought very hard to attain. While today's voices of debate center around lyrics and "crossing over," yesterday's earliest voices were concerned with electric guitars and drums. If you were a church kid in the late sixties and early seventies attending a mostly white, mainline denominational Protestant church, these men were on your side, fighting for your right to plug in a guitar and pound the drums.

Hearn and others had to introduce rock instrumentation slowly and carefully, almost one sound at a time. First it was acoustic guitars (emulating folk music more than rock) with perhaps an electric bass and maybe a tambourine. Later, drums—but not too loud! Then maybe an electric guitar, but certainly not one played through a wah-wah pedal with a big stack of speakers, à la Jimi Hendrix. Carmichael proudly summarized the instrumentation changes they pioneered: "We fought for, and won, the liberty to experiment."

Keep in mind also that this music—the earliest glimmerings of CCM—was introduced to the mainline churches through choir directors. Thousands of churches purchased musical scores of *Good News* and *Tell It Like It Is* in

hopes of putting together a new and exciting contemporary gospel presenta-
tion for their youth-group kids. The only problem, as Hearn relates, was that
"the choir directors were not trained in this music; they were frightened by it."
Carmichael, Hearn, and Kaiser began winning over the Baptists (and others)
by putting on workshops to equip churches for performing musicals.

These pioneers were up against tremendous obstacles. Can you imagine
being frightened by a youth musical? Well, perhaps you can, but I don't think
it's for the same reasons that these choir directors were frightened. Apparently,
CCM's trailblazers had reason for fright a time or two themselves. Carmichael
told me a story about an encounter he had with voices of criticism that were
prevalent at the time:

> Some time after *Tell It Like It Is,* I went up to the National Religious
> Broadcasters convention where I was asked to talk for half an hour
> about my dream to give the kids their own music. I pled for the idea
> that things themselves (electric guitars and drums) are not inherently
> good or evil, that we'd been able to use radio for good, so why not the
> kids' music? Someone stood up and denounced me as "making that
> rock'n'roll sound." Scott Ross, one of the earliest Jesus music DJs, then
> stood up to defend me, but they shouted him down. For a while there
> I thought there might be a stoning.

Despite their struggles, these men had important and influential allies.
Carmichael made it clear that "the Graham organization, Youth for Christ,
and the Southern Baptists were supportive. They said, 'We're gonna try this
'cause it's working with the kids.' "

Although Kaiser, Carmichael, and Hearn went on to write and promote
other youth musicals, the influence of two of the men was just beginning. By
the early 1970s both Ralph Carmichael's Light Records, distributed by Word
Records, and the new Myrrh label, owned by Word and run by Billy Ray

Hearn, were releasing CCM albums by artists such as Randy Matthews and Andrae Crouch and the Disciples. There were other important players entering the field by this time, including Calvary Chapel's Maranatha Records, Larry Norman's Solid Rock label and Bi

Hearn went on to start Sparrow Records in 1976, creating a home for CCM artists Barry McGuire, Keith Green, 2nd Chapter of Acts, and others. Today, Hearn is the chairman of EMI CMG, home to Steven Curtis Chapman, The Newsboys, Stacie Orrico, and many other prominent artists.

THE CONSEQUENCES OF INSUFFICIENT TRUTH

Several of the ideas that fueled the early youth musicals are still with us today. They were ideas important to their time and to cultural change within the church. Yet as comprehensive theologies of music, ministry, and commerce, they are insufficient to the needs of CCM today.

Derivative music, inspired by Up With People for use outside the church to attract the kids, does not give us a sufficient starting place for thinking about music, ministry, or the business of music. Granted, it gets us somewhere, but it is not enough. And it's not enough to prepare us for the future, for faithful integration with culture, or even for faithfully creating music for the church.

Music based on a vision of kids who like pop and rock music, but who need to be "saved" or "discipled," is not music that represents a kingdom perspective. Music with a kingdom perspective allows for this type of use, but in no way is it limited to it. A kingdom perspective has an ideological bias that favors a comprehensive and diverse picture of musical faithfulness. It is music created by musicians called by God, to God, and for God, everywhere, and in everything musical. This is what is meant by a comprehensive view of the role of music in the church and in the culture. It is a huge calling.

Unfortunately, the Baptist influence set the tone for CCM's cultural disengagement from a world infatuated with Mick Jagger and Janis Joplin. We have been hard pressed to recover from this fundamental schism ever since. Christian music became music for "the kids" instead of music for people everywhere and in everything. It emphasized retreating from the cultural sphere by creating a Christian version of popular music just for Christians.

It is biblical and essential to communicate the good news of the kingdom. In this, Billy Ray Hearn, Ralph Carmichael, Kurt Kaiser, Elwyn Raymer, and the Southern Baptist leadership were indeed faithful. All Christians, even the nastiest critics of CCM, must acknowledge that God has used these enthusiastic and imperfect men to add to his church and tell truthful stories. This is reason to give God praise and honor and glory. And it is reason to honor these men and their contributions to the music of the church.

The Jesus and charismatic renewal movements carried with them an urgency to evangelize young people, to tell the truth about Jesus's return for his church, and to initiate fresh experiences of God among young converts. It's biblical and essential to emphasize evangelism, the return of Christ, the worship of God, and the ministry of the Holy Spirit. In this, these movements were tremendously faithful. Here again, all Christians, even the staunchest critics of the Jesus movement and of charismatic experiences, must acknowledge that God used these movements to add to his church and further his kingdom.

The Scriptures on the whole, however, do not teach that a faithful life of following Jesus is constructed only of the evangelism of youth, anticipation of the Rapture, worship services, and hunger for the more extraordinary spiritual gifts. Evangelism is foundational to our mission, and worship and obedience are our only appropriate responses to the gospel, but there is more to the living out of life in Christ and the kingdom mission than these incredibly important ideas support. The models established with the Baptist youth musicals and the Jesus and charismatic renewal movements of the '60s and '70s are insufficient in helping us understand the many ways that one aspect of creation, namely music, can be enjoyed and used in the service of God.

...but what I do

...is that corporate worship, the evangelization of young people, the gifts of the Spirit, and the belief in the imminent return of Jesus were emphasized to such a degree, over and above everything else, that all other ideas seemed small and almost unnecessary by comparison.

CCM, being both a proponent of and partially a result of the Jesus movement, embraced this same set of emphases. As a result, Scriptures and doctrines applicable to CCM and necessary to the construction of a broader, more comprehensive biblical foundation for music in the kingdom at hand were largely overlooked. Few influential people ever widened the lens enough to see music for anything other than a fantastic tool for evangelism, worship, and something for the kids.

I doubt that the pioneers of CCM had any idea their creative choices were laying the foundation for what is today a 500-million-dollar-a-year industry. Had they understood the challenges that lay ahead, it's likely they would have searched the Word for a more complete foundational theology to undergird and influence everything from songwriting, signing artists, and designing album covers to marketing and selling music, staffing companies, and stewarding money. As it was, they did not, and consequently, for more than thirty-five years, contemporary Christian music—the artists, the industry, and the audience—has operated under many of the same insufficient theologies that fueled its beginnings.

When contemporary Christian music began, its ideological and theological influences were very limited. The Baptist influence was mostly one of a denomination loosely defining a mission and opening up the door to possibilities that CCM founders such as Billy Ray Hearn ably walked through. And while it's true that the Jesus and charismatic renewal movements of the late '60s did touch a diverse group of Christians, including Catholics and Episcopalians, no group of believers felt their influence more than the nondenominational church—the worshiping environment of choice for many of CCM's founders.

The Checks and Balances of Diversity

A lack of diverse influences in contemporary Christian music has contributed to a shortage of checks and balances that the body of Christ is designed to provide in everything related to its mission. One of the most important doctrines found in the biblical Story is the doctrine of the body of Christ, which affirms that the church is indeed a diverse group of people and that we need each other's diversity to be healthy. CCM's lack of diversity begs this question: While the Southern Baptists, along with many nondenominational charismatics, were opening their arms to the new contemporary-sounding Jesus music, where were the other denominations? The Billy Graham organization was there, along with various important campus ministries, but where were the other followers of Jesus who placed a high premium on the Bible as the central voice in a believer's life? Unfortunately, they were largely absent from any charitable, meaningful, ongoing dialogue concerning the creation of CCM, its mission, and its infrastructure. If the errors and sins of CCM's primary founders were in building an industry upon narrow and insufficient ideological and theological bedrock, then the errors and sins of those absent from any influence or dialogue are of the "omission" variety—they didn't show up to contribute.

Even though the deconstruction of biblical authority was good reason to avoid many of the mainline denominations in the '60s, there were men and women who could have helped CCM flesh out a more comprehensive and faithful understanding of music, ministry, and commerce. With the exception of Francis and Edith Schaeffer and a small handful of others, very few of them brought comprehensive theologies to bear upon contemporary culture or upon the early dialogues regarding contemporary Christian music, or music and faith in general.

Conservative Presbyterians and, in particular, those of the Reformed tradition (the tradition of Luther, Calvin, and the Puritans) could have contributed to CCM a reasonably fleshed-out theology of vocation or calling. Some in this tradition could have spoken to music's utilitarian use as well as to the Christian's freedom to simply enjoy music as a gift from God. Others could have offered the truth that Christians are free and called to enter into the musical dialogue of culture *and* faithfully contribute biblically sound and aesthetically beautiful music to the church. In short, the knowledge necessary for formulating a comprehensive kingdom perspective of music was within our reach.

Failure to Walk the Talk

Various problems kept these Reformed thinkers from having any kind of measurable influence. One problem was a general arrogance on the part of those who could have contributed—an arrogance that dismissed the importance of pop culture. This turning-up-of-the-nose at the counterculture and the music of youth was a huge miscalculation. The result was a general failure to anticipate the kind of impact these forces would b...

...ly tuned theologies of art and music, work and calling, many of these believers were at a loss about how to live out these ideas and ideals in the world between Sundays. In the eyes of the average young person not following Jesus, most of these mainline believers appeared to be just as sold out to empty platitudes, shallow lives, and relentless materialism as their unbelieving neighbors. More often than not, these traditional models also lacked the vitality and enthusiasm that always accompany the joy of being known by Jesus and being commissioned as a co-worker in the kingdom. I think this was the main reason Jesus people and the charismatic nondenominational churches often referred to many such believers, their churches, their denominations, and their theology as being "spiritually dead." Their apparent dullness and conformity were very substantial reasons why the vitality and excitement of the new charismatic nondenominational fellowships held such an attraction for new young converts. As I noted earlier, they felt that God was not about to pour new wine into old wineskins.

Suspicious Minds

Another important reason for the lack of ideological and theological integration between CCM's primary founders and other possible contributors was an unfortunate suspicion of one another. Anyone vocal about laying claim to a theology rooted in the Reformed theology of Luther and Calvin was automatically suspect in the eyes of the average charismatic nondenomina-tionalist. This reaction was due in large part to an enculturated misunder-standing of the Reformed view of predestination and its relationship to evan-gelism (see Romans 8:29-30). While reformers say we can evangelize with confidence because God has predestined people to be saved, charismatics often viewed Reformed types as being lax on evangelism—"since God has predes-tined, why bother evangelizing?" This misunderstanding led to a general cari-cature of Reformed theology as being antievangelistic. The principal founders of CCM, who placed a high priority on evangelism, often viewed brothers and sisters in the Reformed tradition as ivory-tower thinkers who were far more committed to arguing over doctrine than saving sinners.

In like manner, many mainline churches and teachers, including those of the Reformed faith, were strongly suspicious of the Jesus people, the charis-matic nondenominational churches, and their evangelists and teachers. In his popular book *Dynamics of Spiritual Life,* Richard Lovelace noted,

> Critics of the Jesus people have included not only liberals upset by
> Neo-Fundamentalism but also Evangelical spokesmen who have
> attacked the shallow theology and sensational tactics of the movement's
> leaders and vigorously repudiated its claims to be the onset of a major
> spiritual awakening.[1]

Men and women within the mainline denominations, keepers of rich theological traditions, frequently reduced Jesus-movement charismatics to holy-roller caricatures. Throughout the history of CCM, both camps have been less than kind to one another. Instead of bringing tensions, criticisms, and disagreements to light in charitable dialogue, they have more often than not resorted to backstabbing and throwing stones—often with full media coverage.

SOMETHING'S MISSING

What's missing from CCM is a comprehensive theology of music in general,
and a theology of CCM

Christians, particularly young Christians, often dismiss theology because
they feel no need for it. According to artist Wes King, "When we say *theology*,
there are automatically going to be those people who say 'Oh, those egg-
heads.' " King goes on to say that theology "can have bad connotations when
it becomes a pedantic approach composed of rights and wrongs and lists of
rules. I think there's credence in criticism of this variety of theology."[2]

It's time for us to remember what true theology is, because depending on
feeling over thinking leaves us reaching for the world's ideas when we really
need to apply a kingdom perspective to every subject under the sun. It is impossible in the kingdom at hand to come up with an exhaustive theology, but a
sufficient theology is not beyond our grasp.

Defining Theology

At its simplest and truest, theology is God-thoughts, God-knowledge, or the
study of God-thoughts. Since every cognizant person has some thought or
opinion about God, he or she possesses a theology of some kind, good or bad.
According to J. I. Packer, "God-thoughts are only right when they square with
God's own thoughts about himself; theology comes good only when we let
God's revealed truth—that is, Bible teaching—penetrate our minds."[3] Wes
King makes the musical connection: "If we don't hate what God hates and

love what he loves and hope for what he hopes for, then we're going to have bad theology, bad music, shallow music, and we're probably going to look more to what the world is doing."

Unfortunately, there's no "probably" about it. It is what we do. From music to marketing, CCM takes its cues from the world. This is due in part to the fact that CCM has many leaders who simply will not lead, either out of fear or for lack of a sufficient theology for their calling. "What often happens," Os Guinness says, "is that Christians wake up to some incident or issue and suddenly realize they need to analyze what's going on. Then having no tools of their own, they lean across and borrow the tools nearest them."[4] On this point, Scott MacLeod's prophecy appears to be correct: "The people who have been in power have, knowingly or unknowingly, let the ways of the world enter into Christian music."[5] I do not know if this is because powerful evil spirits plague and control much of the Christian music industry, as MacLeod claims God has revealed to him they do. What I do know is that Christian leaders who attempt to lead without having committed to the ongoing development of a sufficient theology are cooperating with the overall mission of antigood, spiritual powers in the world—including the king of liars, Satan himself. The practical effect is that the disciples they make along the way are no better equipped than they are.

If Satan cannot have the eternal life of a person—and he can't—then he will at least try to see to it that a follower of Jesus lives an ineffective and unproductive life. He must acquiesce to the fact that followers of Jesus are kingdom people, but he doesn't have to make it easy for people to cultivate a comprehensive kingdom perspective—and he doesn't.

To operate under an insufficient theology, above all else, is to possess too few of God's thoughts about himself, people, and place. When a theology is constructed of too many God-thoughts that don't square with the Bible, that theology is insufficient. Also insufficient are theologies constructed of misapplied truth (when good and true ideas are not used in the manner or context for which they were intended).

A sufficient theology is one composed of God-thoughts regarding every area of life, carefully checked against and constructed of God's thoughts as revealed in his Word (and specifically in the person of Jesus). This comprehensive and sufficient theology is ~~~~~~~~~~~~~

.............ity and keeps it from living out a comprehensive version of the Christian mission in the kingdom at hand. Without God's thoughts and God's ways, people are left with their own dim and insufficient ideas. If professing followers of Jesus willfully choose to neglect the work of building truthful theologies for their callings, they will find themselves stumbling blindly down the way that seems right to them but leads to nothing but darkness.

Theology informs mission. A mission without good theology is no mission at all, regardless of whether your mission is good business or good vocational ministry. Here, leaders in the CCM community must take special note. A man or woman in leadership who fails to make the connection between good theology and good business is one who has yet to enter into the fullness of what it means to lead. Faithfulness for a Christian businessperson is not defined solely by faithfulness to good stewardship principles. Granted, stewardship urges us to make the most of what we receive. If this results in increased profits, it's a good thing. However, we can only call it truly good when the means and methods of achieving the profit have not violated God's prescribed ways of being human that are found in Jesus. In order for people to get near this goal, God's good thoughts must precede good business. The best of good business always begins with God's notion of good. The only way to get at his ideas regarding good is to know what he has said. The only place to faithfully get at what he has spoken is the biblical Story.

Theology Lite

I once heard of a young band who, in an attempt to appear relevant to the prevailing Christian culture, declared that they were "into Jesus, but without all the theological baggage." The point I hope to make is that it's impossible to be into Jesus and not be into theology. Every believer has a theology whether or not he or she recognizes it or can articulate it, whether or not it is cogent, real, truthful, and sufficient. This being the case, the goal of the CCM community ought to be to pursue the most faithful understanding possible of the biblical Story and its application to life.

There is a contingent of believers who would like to see knowledge—the thinking component—relegated to a much smaller role in the construction of Christian theology. To quote David Wells, they desire a theology in which "any cognitive elements are strained through the sieve of what appears to be 'practical,' so that what is felt becomes as important as what is known or believed."[6] Wells goes on to identify this reconfiguration of theology as therapeutic.

There are many sincere CCM artists who would declare with a hint of pride that their mission is not to present music that causes people to think so much as to feel, and specifically to feel that everything's going to be all right. God's in the driver's seat, so don't give up hope—keep your eyes on the prize. This approach is indeed therapeutic in that it ministers to the felt needs of the audience. Rather than wrestling with what they've yet to grasp, it reminds the audience over and over of what they learned in the first week of being a Christian.

Certainly music reaches the emotions, and reaching emotions and relieving anxiety is not necessarily a bad thing. The problem, however, lies in thinking that making people feel good about being a Christian or relieving pain and anxiety is the ultimate focus and purpose of Christian music. Especially problematic are songs that stress to listeners that they made the right choice by becoming a Christian and that they need to just hang in there—everything's going to be all right; Jesus is on the case.

One popular group that's come to realize there is a bigger, more serious reality at stake is Point of Grace. "I think God is putting this urgency in all of us," says group member Shelley Breen, "to see that what we're doing with our group is more serious than we ever thought it was. We've always taken it seri-ously, but in the ~~~ ~

~~~~~~~~ DISAGREEMENTS?

This discussion of the importance of cultivating a comprehensive theology is not meant to infer that all Christians must be in agreement on all things at all times. We will certainly have differences of opinion when it comes to theology and its doctrinal particulars, but this does not mean we should avoid formu-lating convictions on debatable issues. As author Mark Shaw points out, "Though these other [debatable] matters are secondary to the primary truths of salvation, they cannot be ignored, because they are addressed in the Word of God."[8]

It is our responsibility to know the Word of God and to seek, as best we can, to formulate truthful and informed ideas about what the Word says and how its teaching applies to our primary and secondary callings. Inevitable dif-ferences of opinion never excuse us from the work of being students of the Word. Followers of Jesus should always seek to understand ever more truth and remain open to the possibility that we have misunderstood some portion of Scripture.

Bringing differences to light can be profitable. This process helps us iden-tify what is complementary in our thinking. It can also help us refine our posi-tions and give careful consideration to whether someone else's position might be more accurate than our own.

Most important, we should never forget that theology—God's thoughts and what we glean from the study of them—are meant to serve the church and the creation. None of us who truly loves the church and God's creation can afford to become so attached to our personal theological formulations that we forget theology is meant to be used as an act of love and service to the church and the watching world.

People for whom theology is a vocational calling wisely recognize that the training and ability to rightly divide the Word of God is God's gift to them, and all God's good gifts are to be used for the building up of the church. All the rest of us, the "little theologians," also need to recognize that our theologies ultimately make up our ideas about what we think it means to be a student-follower of Jesus, how life is to be approached, and how we should live out our calling to music everywhere and in everything. To the degree we think biblically sound thoughts about artistry, industry, and the role of the audience, we proportionately increase our chances of living as biblically informed and faithful people.

Good Theology as a Response to God

Finally, developing truthful and comprehensive theologies is a way of responding in love to God. Jesus said that the first and greatest commandment is to "love the Lord your God with all your heart and with all your soul and with all your mind" (Matthew 22:37). This is the starting place, our primary calling. Only by beginning here will we ever be able to fulfill the second greatest commandment, our secondary calling to "love your neighbor as yourself" (Matthew 22:39). Loving God's thoughts and loving his kingdom story of creation, redemption, and re-creation are what spark the spiritual imagination to dream well and choose well for the church, for the creation, and for your neighbors who make up the watching world. Living in loving response to God, who first loved us, absolutely defines the Christian life, and as such, ought to define contemporary Christian music, and any music created by those stumbling after Jesus. To think this way is to have a good theology. To do it, to live it out, is to live in response to God's love. It is to show that you clearly understand the theology you profess. You are making the invisible kingdom of God visible to the world. Thi

We can see that evangelism was a core priority for those involved in CCM's genesis. Since those simple and zealous beginnings, a complex multimillion-dollar industry has developed. In the process, many Christians have worried and wondered if artists and industry executives have strayed from their original mission. Others have questioned whether evangelism is even a valid priority in an industry where the majority of consumers are already believers.

In this chapter we'll take a look at the methods and ideologies regarding evangelism that have developed since the CCM industry's inception in the '60s and '70s.

The Backstory on Modern Evangelism

I'll begin by saying that modern evangelical ideas regarding evangelism are present within CCM. By "modern evangelical ideas," I don't mean ideas of the present day as much as ideas that began with the Second Great Awakening in the early 1800s and, in particular, with the preacher Charles Finney. Finney's evangelistic technique represents an important shift in the history of Christian evangelism and revivals. His invitation to people to become Christians employed evangelistic techniques and organized meetings that stirred emotions and called for public commitments. From that point forward, many evangelicals have allowed this methodology to define and inspire their ideas regarding evangelism.

This influence is strange in that it is so disconnected from the methods and agenda of Jesus. The invitation Jesus extended to his student-followers was one of forgiveness and authentic humanity and community, an invitation dependent on God the Father drawing people to him. Jesus invited people to hear his word and watch his work. He told stories about what constituted reality for the human family, and he showed that the presence of the kingdom meant the presence of health in every area of life—the rule and reign of the true King of kings made known. Jesus's work was to reconcile humans with God and creation, especially with one another. Jesus invited people to become participants in his kingdom where forgiveness of sin is standard behavior, and love is the measure of all activity. His way of being human, of telling the story of life, of bringing healing to a broken world resonated with human hearts, and people followed him as his students. The passionate work of his Cross is still drawing people to him. Life was his evangelism, not religious techniques. There is much to say about this, but it will have to suffice to say that modernity's need to speed up processes and to promise results fueled the embrace of evangelistic techniques over community embodiment of the Jesus way.

Artists past and present, from Rez Band, Keith Green, and Mylon LeFevre to Carman, NewSong, and FFH have maintained a modern evangelistic focus in that they have offered audiences an invitation to become Christians at the end of concerts, much as Finney offered an invitation at the end of his revivals. It's likely that artists are modeling their methods more after Billy Graham than Charles Finney, but even Graham's evangelistic approach is in this tradition.

Presence Versus Priority

One problem in the debate and criticism about evangelism in CCM is the failure to distinguish between *presence* and *priority* and to understand what the

dominant priorities of CCM actually are. While the kind of modern evangelism mentioned above is present in CCM, it is not a priority for CCM as an
industry. I believe that as a complex organizational system, the industry's main
priorities are to:

.... and to fund the recording, promotion, market-
ing, and distribution of their music, their artistry, and their ministry
to the Christian community.

3. Support all the components and players within the infrastructure of
the CCM system, including producers, songwriters, musicians,
recording studios, engineers, graphic artists, photographers, publishers, parachurch ministries, talent agencies, attorneys, managers, concert promoters, writers, critics, retail stores, youth pastors, and all
forms of media, such as print, television, radio, and the Internet, to
the end that the ministry, recorded product, and live performances of
Christian artists reach Christian consumers in numbers significant
enough to sustain industry.

While there are, of course, exceptions to these priorities, most people
operating within the CCM system will find them to be an accurate description of industry goals. Artists with other priorities (such as evangelism) can
certainly be financially successful in the CCM industry as long as the results
of their work overlap to an extent with the goals stated above—particularly the
goal of reaching the Christian consumer base. Whether these artists will feel
emotionally or spiritually satisfied while working within this context is another
matter entirely.

Certainly, creating music for the church is vitally important, and the impetus to do so is driven by such powerful ideas as love and stewardship. Even so, the question remains as to what, if anything, reaching a Christian consumer base has to do with evangelism—either as Finney defined it or as Jesus lived it.

Preaching to the Choir

If CCM artists show themselves to be evangelizing out of sincere and faithful hearts, this will in no way stop "born-again" Christians from attending their concerts. On the contrary, it's likely that more Christians will attend. The CCM community understands this phenomenon and uses it to its advantage. Christian music and evangelism have a long history of coexistence, and many churches, pastors, artists, industry folks, and fans in the audience still like it that way—even though it is, essentially, more rhetoric than spiritual reality. Many churches, youth pastors, and promoters have come to expect evangelism at a Christian concert, even one primarily attended by Christians. If this seemingly contradictory expectation goes unfulfilled, it stirs up voices of criticism. Remember these words from the WAY-FM open letter? "In our opinion, the gospel also has been diluted to some degree in live concerts. We have been disappointed in the last few years with some of the concerts our stations have promoted. In some instances, there has been little or no ministry throughout the entire event." These comments represent the thoughts of a great many Christians on the importance of an evangelistic appeal in a Christian concert.

Because of the potential diversity of people reading this book, I think some definition of *evangelism* is in order. For example, the word *evangel*, from the Greek word *euangelion*, means "good news." This definition relates directly to Jesus and his announcement of the new kingdom way: " 'The time has come,' he said. 'The kingdom of God is near. Repent and believe the good news!' " (Mark 1:15). To repent means to give up your agenda for life and begin to live in light of the new opportunity Jesus announced. What is this new opportunity? It is to be reconciled to God through Messiah Jesus, to become human as God designed you to be—an unceasing spiritual being, a coparticipant with God in the care of his creativity, and a member of a world-wide tribe of people throughout ......

...relationship model of invitation and gravitate instead toward the propositional model in which various assertions about reality are stated and the audience is asked to agree to them. Those who agree raise their hands or walk down an aisle where evangelism counselors, pastors, or priests pray for them.

With this type of evangelism, a Christian record company faces neither difficulty nor risk in supporting artists who utilize these methods. In fact, supporting these artists helps record companies maneuver through the maze of contradictions that the evangelism issue has become. In good conscience, record companies can tell pastors, artists, parents, and fans that nothing has changed and that the companies continue to be strong advocates of music and evangelism—as they have always been. And here's why:

1. CCM record companies know that Christians attend Christian concerts even when evangelism is emphasized. Some come precisely because it is. This fulfills the record companies' priority of getting the music to their core consumers.

2. CCM record companies know that some portion of the Christian audience will bring unbelieving friends, neighbors, and relatives to hear a gospel appeal. This fulfills, in part, the need of Christian men and women inside the record companies to get involved in evangelism. It affirms to them that they are doing something that has eternal value.

3. CCM record companies know that some portion of the audience will be composed of children and teenagers who attend church with their Christian parents but have yet to come to a saving faith in Messiah Jesus. A Christian concert where the gospel is proclaimed is yet one more opportunity for these children and teenagers to acknowledge Christ as their Savior. As in point two, this helps fulfill the need of Christian men and women inside record companies to involve themselves, if only indirectly, in evangelism as they understand it. And again, they feel an affirmation that their labor has eternal value.

The Christian Concert: Tricks or Truth?

From CCM's inception, concerts have been used as a tool to draw unbelievers to an event where the good news will be preached—an approach I've long referred to as the music-as-magnet method. Peter Furler of the Newsboys understands this reality but makes it quite clear that such methodology does not represent his own thinking:

> You might find someone who totally believes with all their heart that our music is meant to draw kids along so we can preach to them. To be honest, I have never ever thought that in my life, in my whole fifteen years of being on the road with a band playing music. I've heard preachers tell us that when we've done a crusade or a tent revival, saying, "I'm glad you're here, the music, bringing the young people along."[1]

However, an unbeliever of any age will seldom be drawn to CCM-styled evangelistic concerts without an invitation from a believing friend or relative. The believer who invites an unbeliever to a Christian music concert bets on the entertainment value of music to entice the unbeliever to attend. The fact that the gospel will be preached at the event is more often than not left as a surprise, something Phil Joel of the Newsboys takes exception to.

> I think there is a little bit of dish

The approach of inviting unsaved friends and relatives to a Christian concert is similar in many ways to that taken by people who attend a Billy Graham crusade. There are some distinct differences though. With Dr. Graham, music is not necessarily the draw, and the gospel message is featured rather than downplayed, hidden, or relegated to five minutes in a ninety-minute event. Most unbelievers who attend a Graham crusade know ahead of time that a preacher, albeit the world's most famous one, is going to preach to them about salvation in Christ alone. Due in no small part to Graham's sterling reputation, people willingly come to his crusades, and by God's grace they walk out new men and women, eager to embrace the kingdom opportunity. My wife's mother came to faith in Jesus this way.

Most artists who evangelize in the Christian concert setting do so with full knowledge that the audience before them is largely composed of people who already know and love Christ. Because of this, artists who evangelize within CCM will sometimes announce ahead of time that their concert tour will have an evangelism emphasis. This alerts Christians to bring along their unbelieving family, friends, or acquaintances. Armed with the assurance that "unsaved" children and adults are present in the audience, the artist faithfully makes an appeal for the gospel. This is the attitude and approach that has characterized the popular group NewSong.

"The bad news," explains NewSong member Eddie Carswell, "is that our ministry is more of an inreach. We're about a bunch of different things. We're encouraging the guy out in row eight, we're about getting people to support kids through World Vision, and we're in prisons. As far as the evangelistic side, if that's all we're about, we should be down at Wal-Mart on a flatbed, probably."[3]

Some well-meaning pastors, churches, and promoters who are intently involved with the Christian music community have yet to realize that Christian concerts are primarily the domain of Christians. In various interviews for this book, I quickly discovered that CCM artists and bands encounter promoters who have wholly unreasonable expectations about evangelism, especially about the nature and fruit of the "altar call." In 1998 the band Small Town Poets told me a story that I think epitomizes the altar-call experience for many Christian musicians:

> Our ire was raised a little bit when a concert promoter sent back our manager's concert follow-up evaluation sheet, and it said, "The altar call was weak, resulting in few decisions." At the end of the show, Miguel took about five minutes to explain the gospel in layman's terms, just as simple as he could. He told them, "That's the gospel; that's what Christ did for you. If you'd like to respond to it, please walk down." Our take on the promoter's comments was this: The gospel can't be weak. It's the good news of Christ. It's salvation to all who believe. All Miguel did was speak it, and if the Holy Spirit moved on people's hearts, it's their responsibility to react. I guess we could have played some piano music, I guess we could have cried, but all we did was present the gospel, and that's not weak. And the fact that he said it resulted in few decisions, well, there were decisions.[4]

Stories like this are not uncommon. Many Christians are still confused about the good work that God has given humans in every sphere of life—

including music. They see it as nothing more than a tool in the evangelism business. The Jesus model of word and work, storytelling and storied living is just not good enough for these people. Yet in the reality of God, it is wholly sufficient and God-honoring to make [text obscured]

[text obscured]

[text obscured] let me make clear how it *doesn't* make sense. But before I do, I should say that this explanation is more of an exercise in critical analysis than a confession of my own opinion in the matter. As you'll read below, I hold a much broader view than the CCM norm of what it means to communicate the good news Jesus spoke of. Nevertheless, I'll dive in.

First, a question. How do you carry out music evangelism when the overwhelming majority of people you're evangelizing are born-again Christians? The answer is, you don't, except in the way described above. Is there anything dreadfully wrong with this approach? I think so, in that it does not square well with the Jesus approach. Yet, I have to yield to the fact that many authentic believers have come to follow Jesus by answering the call of a modern evangelist. Nevertheless, Christian people should not view evangelistic techniques such as altar calls as sufficient or comprehensive. They ought not be fooled into thinking these marketing methods are a substitute for living for God everywhere and in everything, being the word and work of Jesus in the world. Modern evangelism techniques miss that particular mark by a long shot. The gospel is only good news to the neighbor or stranger if it truly is a better, more human way to live. It worries me that people who watch Christians (from the outside looking in) will listen to new converts recite their platitudes, certainties, and propositional truths, and then will see them return to the same life everybody else is living, lives with no distinction, no salt, no light. That would not be attractive, or magnetic. It would not be the pattern of Jesus, and that would be reason for tears.

What the modern evangelistic approach does do is model something that occurs in churches across America every single Lord's Day. Come Sunday, churches fill up with true believers who share the pews with people who feel they are believers but aren't; the occasional curious spiritual seeker doing a taste test; and the relatives, friends, neighbors, and children who come either as guests of Christians or, in the case of children, as required by their parents. Though the salvation message is often preached in church and people do come to understand the good news in a church setting, no Christian who has ever skimmed the Bible believes formal teaching and worship fulfills the Jesus directive to go into the world and make student-followers of all people.

Given this reality, does it make sense for Christian record companies, staffed mostly with Christians, to concentrate on making music solely for Christian consumers? Especially when CCM without a doubt represents the world's largest community of Christian artists involved in the stewardship of music? Doesn't some degree of responsibility come with a well-funded global stewardship? *Billboard* columnist Deborah Evans Price expressed her frustration with these issues: "I can't tell you how many interviews I've asked about mainstream plans for a particular artist or song and get the response that the company is 'exploring options,' and nothing ever happens."[5]

On the surface it makes no sense that Christian record companies would fail to exhaust every opportunity for sending good music into an often dark world. Wouldn't launching God's message of hope and reconciliation into the darkest corners of creation be a priority for anyone who has ever seriously considered the Jesus way? But what if Christian record companies are simply being faithful to their particular calling, a calling that does not necessarily involve taking music created by Christians to the mainstream music lover? What if, like the apostle Paul before them, Christian record companies are being faithful to their calling, doing the good they know to do in the CCM arena and not wanting to duplicate or build upon the good work that Christian brothers and sisters are already doing in mainstream music (see Romans 15:20)? If this is justifiably the case, then many critics of CCM's narrow focus have no basis for criticism

...work related to Christian music is most God-honoring. Inwardly, many within CCM grieve that Christians aren't more involved with the stewardship of music everywhere and in everything. Yet most stay within the system and use CCM as a base to make broader contributions. Eddie Carswell referred to using his platform with NewSong to minister in prisons or to get people interested in World Vision. Such service to people is good and leads to good. Unfortunately for many people, steering the ship of Christian music to other equally good ports of entry (far beyond the range of CCM) feels like an overwhelming and impossible task the majority of the time. As a result, many new musicians and business people are abandoning or ignoring Christian music altogether. There is a sense among this new tribe that the system is too flawed and too far gone to be set straight. People are sick of CCM's limited view of the use and enjoyment of music, and even smaller view of what it means to tell a life-altering story, to communicate good news. They are not in the evangelism business of old. They do not believe that music is only a tool for evangelism. They actually believe that music is a legitimate God-blessed vocation. They believe that the best way to evangelize is by showing others that following Jesus is a better way to live.

William Romanowski is correct in his observation that when CCM began, "it justified its existence and activities on the assumption that contemporary popular music was an effective vehicle for bringing the evangelical message of personal salvation through Christ to the modern youth culture and promoting 'traditional' beliefs and values."[6]

Romanowski is also correct when he writes that CCM's pioneers believed a "fusion of marketing and ministry would simultaneously save souls and generate profits." However, the fruit of the fusion has been that "evangelism became the industrial rhetoric, not the spiritual reality."[7] This has never been more true than it is today. The story that Christian music generally communicates about what it means to be a student-follower of Jesus is tragically too small. Its fundamental and popular communication of the good news is not good news. If it were, it would attract more people outside the church. If it were, people in the industry would die to have the world experience it. Christian music has succeeded in creating a completely separate genre of music while failing to delight ears with great music and the best and most important story about what it means to be God's people in this world.

7

History shows that disagreement and debate over musical matters in the church are not unique to our time, or to the CCM community. Christians have long debated the theological content of lyrics and the issue of musical accompaniment—whether congregational singing should be supported by musical instruments, and if so, what kind of instrumentation and what style of accompaniment is appropriate. For many Christians, issues of style and instrumentation have either been resolved or are no longer as volatile as they once were, and in light of the commercialization and popularity of contemporary Christian music, other more complex issues have surfaced. In this chapter, we will address questions about the use and purpose of music itself.

Most of us hold various biases when it comes to music. That's perfectly reasonable. The only qualification for a bias, conviction, or opinion is knowing and understanding what compels us to hold it. In other words, my conviction or opinion starts to become good only when I know why I believe it. That knowledge begins with the biblical Story and the testimony of creation, not with my gut. If I lean toward a gut feeling, a little too much pizza the night before might very well cause me to hold some very strange convictions. I must know and understand what compels me to take the position I do, and I must be ready to wrestle with any possible contradictions regarding the uses of music in my own personal life.

As the CCM voices in chapter 1 indicate, some artists believe that "music, by Biblical definition, is a ministry." Others would say that because music is familiar to everyone, it is useful as a tool for winning young people to Jesus and discipling them in their spiritual journey. Others say that the best thing we can do with our music is to praise God, but they also add that God created music in such a way that it is good and useful for communicating important thoughts and emotions in a variety of settings and for a variety of purposes.

Here's where the battle is joined. If music is indeed the powerful tool many say it is, they can't leave it idle when there's a job to do. If something powerful is not accomplishing its powerful purpose, then its power is being wasted. If people feel strongly about the waste, they're likely to feel anger, regret, grief, or frustration. They're ready to pledge to God and the church to do all they can to prevent future waste and misuse. In similar fashion, those who believe that the musical energies of God's people should be spent, with very few exceptions, on praise and worship, evangelism, and discipleship will likely feel anger and frustration when that energy is redirected.

A sincere commitment to the position that music created by Christians must *do* something fuels much of the criticism that sounds out in our community. Voices such as these are not alone in their zeal to protect powerful tools. History shows that Jesus's disciples also shared this propensity.

Jesus and the Beautiful Thing

Jesus was in Bethany at the home of a man known as Simon the Leper. While Jesus reclined at Simon's table, a woman named Mary came and stood behind Jesus and began to weep. She carried a pint of very expensive perfume. As her tears began to drip down upon the feet of Jesus, Mary took the alabaster jar of perfume and poured it on his head and his feet, mixing the perfume with her tears. Kneeling down, she kissed Jesus's feet and wiped them with her hair. When the disciples saw this, they grumbled indignantly among themselves, saying, "What a waste of perfume." One disciple

[text obscured]

intentions, many of us become consumed by an overwhelming need to shape and control the uses of music for what we truly believe to be admirable purposes. Often our voices, like the disciples' voices, are fueled by the heartfelt desire to see some perceived wrong made right. Our error is in trying to right a wrong that is not wrong and therefore does not need to be fixed. Instead of building up and helping those who want to do a beautiful thing for Jesus, we often grumble and tear them down for their seeming lack of practicality.

The disciples misunderstood the economy of God. Though every one of us should remain open to the good and practical uses of music, we need to guard ourselves against repeating the errors of the first disciples. We want to remain open to the idea that Jesus may be saying to some of us even now, "Dear friend, leave this sister's music alone. Why are you bothering her? She has done a beautiful thing to me."

Second, not only do we want to remain open to this possibility, we want to be very careful to avoid the sin of Judas. In John 12:6, Scripture teaches that Judas was upset about the waste of perfume not because "he cared about the poor but because he was a thief; as keeper of the money bag, he used to help himself to what was put into it." Judas saw the perfume as a means to a selfish end, yet he pretended to be concerned with a higher and better use of it.

The Starting Place

God saw fit to include music in the totality of his creation, and as such it needs no further justification. This is the starting place for thinking about music, period.

For many people in and around CCM, this bedrock truth is very difficult to accept. Because so much has been accomplished using music in the ways common to contemporary Christian music, the thought of freely using music in other ways seems to many people unfaithful or willfully disobedient. In reality, it's when we fail to think in other ways that we risk being found unfaithful. Our musical calling is for God's purposes, which are vast. Faithfulness equals God's people and their music everywhere and in everything. I strongly believe that until this idea is understood and owned, clear thinking on the enjoyment and use of music will continue to elude our community.

A final note: In the course of framing this argument, I may have given the impression that I'm bent on advocating and encouraging CCM to let the music be—and that's all. On the contrary, what I hope to communicate is that God's people are called to do the beautiful thing in every sphere of life, and that looking for practical applications for any part of creation, including CCM, is not the place to start with our thinking about the stewardship of music. We are free to let it be, and we are free to use it responsibly.

THE GLORIOUS FREEDOM OF THE CHILDREN OF GOD

Music needs no justification for its existence; it is a priceless gift from God that we can use for good and productive purposes. Music is not transformed into something good when crafty humans discover some good use for it. This is an important distinction that must be understood by every reader, from parents to pastors to pop stars. Creation is useful *because* it is good. It is not good just because it is useful.

The good mind of God has created good things, music included, because

God is nothing less than good. This is the starting place for thinking Christianly about the use of everything God has created. If Christians fail to start their thinking at this point, they risk falling into the error of the pragmatist. A pragmatist believes that something is good or ~~ ~~ ~~ is useful. Prag~~~~~~

~~~~cause ~~~~ for good, but there is no guarantee ~~ fallen creatures will always use them that way.

One way to think of music as being good on its own, even if it isn't "doing anything," is to compare it with another of God's creations: water. Because water is good, it's useful. Yet despite its many important uses, I'm free to hike along a stream high in the Rocky Mountains of Colorado and enjoy the beauty of the water without ever making any practical use of it. Because it's there does not mean that I must harness it for some use. On the contrary, I can find pleasure in the water alone. I can let it be and in so doing find pleasure in God's good creation. In the beauty of the stream, I recognize God's handiwork, and I give him thanks and praise for it.

Genesis 1:26-30 teaches that as image-bearers of God and as followers of Jesus, we are caretakers and stewards of the planet, including the planet's water. Part of our work on the planet is to take care of what God has created—water, music, and everything else. No one gets off the hook.

All people involved with CCM, including the audience, need to understand the role freedom plays in the enjoyment and use of God's creation of music. In grace we have the freedom to say no to every form of ungodliness as well as the freedom to say yes to our growing and compelling desire to live for God everywhere and in everything. We can reject all ideas that claim the enjoyment of creation and its pleasures leads people away from godliness and should therefore be avoided. These ideas are an affront to God's imaginative creativity (see 1 Timothy 4:4) and a challenge to the truthfulness of his Word (see Genesis 1 and 1 Timothy 4:1-5).

The freedom to use and enjoy all of creation is qualified by the higher freedom of love. Love compels us to keep watch over our exercise of freedom so we don't cause weaker brothers and sisters to stumble (see 1 Corinthians 8:7-13). Love compels us to remember that while "everything is permissible...not everything is beneficial" (1 Corinthians 6:12). The biblical Story also reminds us that our freedom can be misused. History teaches us that we have the intrinsic potential to choose very poorly on behalf of something very good, music included. The themes of freedom and servanthood work together in a pact of strength, as reflected in Galatians 5: "You, my brothers, were called to be free. But do not use your freedom to indulge the sinful nature; rather, serve one another in love. The entire law is summed up in a single command: 'Love your neighbor as yourself'" (verses 13-14).

If our freedom in Christ is governed and defined by love and service, then our freedom to use and enjoy music in a variety of ways ought to be guided by these qualities as well. Only the most wide-ranging view of what it means to love will work here, though. Loving you might require my writing a song to remind you of truths you've forgotten or neglected. Loving you might require writing an instrumental melody for you that is remarkably beautiful in order to remind you of your need for beauty.

Now for the qualifications: While we're free to enjoy water and find pleasure in it apart from any practical use it may have, we're not free to use it for something unworthy of its inherent good. We've said that because water is good, it contains the potential for good use. We've also considered the fact that Christians are free, but we shouldn't use our freedom as a cover-up for sin or for indulging the sinful bias within us—a bias that urges us to live contrary to the integrity we possess as new creations in Christ.

We can use water sinfully. I remember when the phrase *wet T-shirt contest* became part of the cultural lexicon. I've never attended such a contest, but any kid who's ever gone swimming with a T-shirt on knows what happens when a T-shirt gets wet: It clings to your skin, and your skin shows through. As I understand it, these contests ~~

~~ good of water, the good of human sexuality, and the good image within each human. Neither water nor human beings are made for such foolishness. The freedom to enjoy creation, whether it be water or the beautiful form of a woman, is not the freedom to choose sin. It is the freedom to love and to serve. In the example above, there's no evidence of love or servanthood. There's only evidence of sinful self-interest, which is always the bias of sin. Indulging the sin bias within always involves violating the integrity of creation.

Doing the Good You Know to Do

While I'm free to enjoy a mountain stream for its beauty, I'm not free to ignore the good uses the stream may have. One of those uses might be to feed the reservoir of a dam that creates hydroelectric power for surrounding towns and cities. If those with the foresight to imagine hydroelectric power had balked at pursuing this invention, knowing full well the good it could contribute to people's lives, they would have been guilty of willfully choosing to ignore a good use for water.

Today, if I hike a stream in order to enjoy its beauty, yet pollute it with trash from my lunch, I am guilty of ignoring one good use of the stream—keeping trout alive. As an avid fisherman and a caretaker of the planet, I have a vested interest in seeing trout flourish. I should know that trashing a stream will have an adverse effect on its ecosystem. When I fish, I prefer the catch-and-release technique. In other words, I don't eat the fish; I put them back in the stream. At present I don't need trout for food. However, someday I may, and I won't be pleased to discover that my abuse of freedom has threatened a good, God-provided food source.

If I become thirsty after hours of hiking along my private Colorado trout stream (sorry, the hopeful dreamer in me came out), the stream can now meet a very legitimate need. God created my body to require water, and without it I will not live. I'm now free to drink from the stream to satisfy this need. When I drink from the stream, water, which earlier was a means of visual pleasure and delight, becomes a means of sustaining life. Water moves from something of good enjoyment to something of good use, and in both, God is thanked, praised, and glorified.

A cursory glance at creation reveals that this kind of multifunctioning is all around us and in us. Take a redwood tree, for example. Redwood is great for building homes, outside furniture, and decks because it's resistant to wet weather. As stewards of what God imagined and created, we're free to cut down these trees and use their lumber for countless purposes. Yet, we're also free to create parks for the sole purpose of delighting in the majesty and beauty of these trees. We are free to let them be, and we are free to use them.

Consider human sexuality. Is its function procreation, pleasure, or both? Do you see God's genius in designing creation this way? Look at Scripture for a moment: "And the LORD God made all kinds of trees grow out of the ground—trees that were pleasing to the eye and good for food" (Genesis 2:9). Are human beings both useful and pleasing to the eye? Certainly this is beyond dispute, but just in case, the Bible reminds us that God used Rachel, who "was lovely in form, and beautiful" (Genesis 29:17) as a cobuilder of the house of Israel (see Ruth 4:11).

Music Has Been Left in Our Care

Now let's turn our attention back to music. *Because music is good, it is useful.*
Like water, music also has many uses. H

...usic, and by giving me time to follow Jesus and enjoy his
good gift of music. No apology need ever be made for enjoying the good God
has made (see 1 Timothy 4:4). In music I see God's handiwork, his order, his
design, and I give him thanks and praise for creating it and for giving me the
skill to write and produce it.

Like all of creation, music has been left in our care. Our responsibility is
to enjoy it and make good use of it. But, as with water, we are not free to use
music for something totally unworthy of its inherent good, such as background music in a film promoting hate crimes. While we're free to enjoy
music for its beauty, we're not free to ignore the good uses it may have, such
as "winning young people to Jesus and discipling them in their walk." Music,
like water, can move from something of good enjoyment to something of
good use. Its beauty can soothe the restless soul, and its melody can give flight
to extraordinary words that tell of the Living Water that takes away the thirst
of humankind. In both, God can be thanked, praised, and glorified.

Music can be the melody you whistle while you work; it can be the
melody and lyric that frame a worshipful response to God's grace; and it can
be the sound of a string quartet playing in the background as you walk your
twenty-one-year-old daughter down the aisle. Do you see God's genius in
designing music this way? Does it make you want to praise him? I hope it

does. It should be evident by now that I'm hoping to encourage you to set no limits on music, except those set by the principles of love and servanthood.

As the appointed caretakers of creation, we are to imagine and create music, think of places where music can be of good enjoyment and good use, and support good enjoyment and good use whenever the opportunity arises. We are to put creation to good use by loving and serving others. This emphasis on people does not mean we fail to love and care for creation. It simply means that the good gifts of creation exist to serve God's good purposes for you and me, his image-bearers. In this way people take precedence over the rest of creation. If we see and imagine some good that could potentially come of good music but do not alert others to it or work toward accomplishing it (once we have counted the cost), then we have failed to do the caretaking work God has assigned us.

Getting at the Truth

As I've already pointed out, various voices of criticism have recently brought to the forefront what many people in and around CCM have been saying for thirty years: that music ought to be used for Christian ministry alone. If what these brothers and sisters believe is that the highest and best use of music is for *ministry*, and *music ministry* is defined as music imagined and created in love as a grateful servant's response to God's grace, I am in agreement with them. If their definition of music ministry involves creating music either for the worship of God or for the purpose of serving the church and the watching world as artful salt and light, goodness and truth, then again, I could not agree with them more. They have my full endorsement. This is what music should be.

However, if these voices are saying that the only true and good use of music is to serve the direct needs of the church—either through worship or as a witnessing tool—then I must vigorously speak out against the narrowness of their vision. Christians who advocate and carry out such a narrow vision for music are making a willful choice to relinquish the caretaking role given to humanity. To do this is to turn one's back on the calling. We cannot retreat from the world of music any more than we can retreat from the world of politics, law, education, sports, or medicine. T

...., ... by living good lives among them (see 1 Peter 2:12). Living good lives involves loving our neighbors and giving of ourselves through acts of mercy and kindness (see Mark 12:31; Luke 6:36). The Christian mission involves continued faithfulness to the biblical mandate to care for and manage God's creation, including that part of his creation called music (see Genesis 1:28; Psalm 8:6-8).

In this chapter we've taken a good look at what music is and what our responsibilities and privileges are in relationship to it. We've discussed a follower's freedom in Christ to enjoy music, and we've looked at how loving servanthood defines our uses of it. Next, we come to an issue that has loomed large over the past twenty years: the role and importance of the lyric in contemporary Christian music.

8

In 1991 Amy Grant's *Heart in Motion* album provoked a highly charged discussion of lyric content in the CCM community. Many Christian music leaders and consumers did not know what to do with an album full of songs about love between men and women. Throughout the 1990s song lyrics from artists such as Sixpence None the Richer and Michael W. Smith were the subjects of debate about what constitutes a Christian song or a Christian record. Industry and audience alike were seeking to determine what music should or should not be played on Christian radio, sold in Christian bookstores, or nominated for the Gospel Music Association's Dove Awards. The development and implementation of "lyric criteria" by gatekeepers at youth ministries, radio stations, and retail stores turned up the flame on an already heated and often divisive discussion.

Tensions regarding lyrics in CCM are lying fairly dormant right now, due in part to the popularity of modern worship music and also to the fact that many young artists who are Christians are bypassing Christian record labels and are taking their music directly to mainstream labels. In addition, shifts in where Christians purchase music have been occurring over the past several years. As more Christian music is sold in general music stores, in the music departments of stores such as Target or Wal-Mart, and on the Internet, Christian bookstores have become somewhat less influential. We will look at these developments in later chapters, but here let's explore some issues related to lyrics in contemporary Christian music.

THE BURDEN OF PROOF

Contemporary Christian music is an unusual genre. Every other form of popular music is classified by its musical style: jazz, blues, classical, folk, rap, and rock. Contemporary Christian music incorporates all these styles and more; therefore, it cannot possibly qualify as a genre using the standard means of classification. The only option CCM has is to tie its identification to the lyric, or to a profession of faith by the artists. Years ago a listener might have been able to tell the difference, stylistically, between Christian music and non-Christian music (think Southern gospel quartets versus the Rolling Stones). Today a listener can no longer count on the music to indicate that he or she is indeed listening to Christian music.

This being so, one important function of the contemporary Christian music lyric is to communicate to listeners that they are indeed listening to music that is Christian in origin, and therefore can and should be named accordingly. The most efficient way to achieve this desired end is to incorporate specific names, words, and intrinsically Christian concepts into CCM songs. For example: Jesus, Holy Spirit, redemption, heaven, sin, and glory. Using exclusive language, or at least words common to Christianity, helps Christians and many non-Christians quickly identify the music as Christian in origin.

People must realize, however, that getting listeners to recognize Christian music does not ensure they will engage the music and lyric with the depth of interest necessary to derive some spiritual, emotional, or intellectual benefit from them. Every Lord's Day, Christians around the world sing psalms, hymns, and spiritual songs filled with glorious truths. Yet this does not mean that these truths are penetrating the singers' wandering hearts and minds.

Overtly Christian words work toward ensuring that most listeners will identify the music as Christian. As important as it is for a CCM lyric to achieve
this particular goal, connecting with a listener's personal ideas about Christian
identity and purpose has b

mirrors the prospective buyers' own subjective understandings of Christian
identity and mission. If, for instance, a Christian sees herself primarily as a vic-
tor in Christ (her identity), empowered to overcome the enemy Satan (her
mission), she will naturally identify as "Christian" the music that most accurately reflects her ideas about Christian identity and mission.

While a listener's bias will alert her to lyrics that do not meet her criteria
concerning Christian identity and mission, it will also likely hinder her from
identifying lyrics that may in fact be congruent with a true kingdom perspective of Christian identity and mission. The principle is this: *The smaller and
less comprehensive a person's kingdom perspective or biblical worldview is, the
greater the potential for suspicion and intolerance of lyrics that express a larger,
more comprehensive kingdom perspective.* As unfortunate as this scenario is, it is
made doubly unfortunate when we acknowledge that the potential for suspicion
and intolerance runs both ways. Those who are mature in Christ are sometimes prone to exhibit intolerance for the young, immature, or weak in conscience. This is why the apostle Paul's teaching regarding the weaker brother
and sister ought to undergird our thinking on these topics (see 1 Corinthians 8:1-13; 10:23-33).

A comprehensive kingdom perspective is large enough to hold smaller
views, but the smaller will never hold the larger. For example, a comprehensive kingdom perspective takes into account that God's people are victorious

in and through Messiah Jesus (see 1 Corinthians 15:57; Romans 8:37). However, this is just one small part of the vision. Lyrics written from a kingdom perspective will naturally include a number of topics—in truth an inexhaustible number. On the other hand, a smaller, less comprehensive perspective will usually only include those topics that reflect its bias.

Does It Float?

From the beginning, contemporary Christian music has had to accomplish an assigned task. It could never just be music. It had to serve a religious function that produced a tangible result. The idea that music can also exist as something good, true, and beautiful without having to *do* something is a concept largely foreign to CCM. In truth, the idea that any element of God's creation—be it music or a tree—has to do something in order to justify its existence has more to do with capitalism, consumerism, and marketing than with the doctrine of creation. I don't mean for this to deride the Christian music business community. My desire is simply to draw a fair comparison between what Christian music is most often asked and expected to do and what any other product, whether it's a pair of shoes, a bicycle, or a boat, is expected to do in the marketplace.

The majority of products and services marketed in a capitalistic system are required to do something. For example, if I market something as a boat and yet my so-called boat does not float, it is likely I will soon be out of the boat business. Consumers hold fixed ideas about what they expect in a boat, and above all, they expect it to float. If you decided to shop for a boat at my store, Charlie's Boat and Marine, you might inquire about price, horsepower, and service contracts, but it's unlikely you would ask, "Does this boat float?" Life and circumstances, context, and enculturation have conditioned you to expect that a brand new boat, sold by a legitimate boat dealer, will indeed float. You are so trusting, so confident about it floating, you will purchase it, haul it to a lake, put your cherished family inside it, and take off for a ride in sixty feet of water, without ever having actually confirmed that it floats!

A similar kind of thinking exists with̶ ̶ ̶ ̶ ̶

̶ ̶ ̶ view them as the benchmark criteria for judging the authenticity of music created by Christians. They perceive the slightest movement to the left or the right of these core criteria as failure to advance the very thing they're zealously committed to creating, supporting, marketing, and purchasing.

Now let's plug CCM into my boat story. If I market a recording as Christian music and yet my so-called Christian music does not appear to be "Christian," it is likely I will soon be out of the Christian music business. Consumers hold fixed ideas about what they expect in music labeled Christian, and above all, they expect it to be "Christian." If you shop for Christian music at my store, Charlie's Christian Music & Books, you might inquire about price, style, popularity, and the life and history of the artists represented. But it's unlikely you would pick up a CD and ask me, "Is this one Christian?" Life and circumstances, context, and enculturation have conditioned you to expect that any recording sold by a legitimate Christian music and book store will indeed be "Christian." In truth, most of us are so trusting, so confident about the music being "Christian," we will purchase it, take it home, put it in our CD players, and play it for our cherished family, without actually confirming that it's a Christian recording. We have learned to trust the context or environment in which we make our purchase to be our primary guarantee of Christian authenticity. When consumer expectations are not met, when trust is violated, confidence in a product or service is eroded. This is as true of CCM as it is in any other industry.

WHAT IS A CHRISTIAN LYRIC?

If Christian artists, consumers, and industry people expect Christian music to be "Christian" and see the lyric as the only means by which the song can be identified as "Christian," then what is a Christian lyric? For much of the CCM industry and audience, it is easily defined—and this definition does not allow for the complexity of a kingdom perspective or the new way to be human that Jesus modeled. This is the core issue that drives the debate concerning contemporary Christian music lyrics.

One person hoping to make his easily defined position known is music buyer Rick Anderson, whom you may recall had this to say about Amy Grant's album *Behind the Eyes*: "It's not a Christian album. A Christian album should be clear on the person of Christ, and these lyrics are not." Remember, too, my earlier mention of the two radio networks that declined to play Grant's single "Takes a Little Time." One network cited a lack of "lyrical relevance," and the other a failure to meet "lyrical criteria." Relevant to whom, you might ask, or to what lyrical criteria? For Amy Grant, the relevance of her work is not connected to its ability to meet lyrical criteria. "I don't know if *Behind the Eyes* is a Christian record," Amy says. "Being able to label it Christian or non-Christian is not the point for me. The point was to make available the songs I wrote between 1995 and 1997, and to let them find their own audience."[1]

Here, Amy is at odds with an entire industry and much of its audience—ironically, an industry she helped build and an audience she helped attract. While Amy may not define relevance in terms of meeting lyric criteria, many of her brothers and sisters in CCM do. When a lyric like "Takes a Little Time" comes along and does not clearly communicate Christ (the criteria), it makes sense that many who listen to CCM and work within its community would label such a lyric irrelevant. However, in the case of "Takes a Little Time," the context or environment in which the song is heard contributes most to its being labeled as irrelevant.

Oddly enough, in the big picture of real life, a lyric like "Takes a Little Time" might have a high degree of relevance, if it could be experienced by both Christians and non-Christians in a context other than Christian radio and retail. On the whole, both Christian radio and Christian retail have a very low tolerance for lyrics that deviate from common subject matter they deem relevant to their own biased mission. Lyrics that do not meet their criteria or perpetuate their mission, as they see it, are of little or no use to them. Yet a song like "Takes a Little Time" did garner some Christian radio airplay, partly because of Amy Grant's past reputation for lyrical relevance, and partly because some Christian stations believe in airing the occasional song that addresses social issues or love between two people. In spite of the occasional exception, the voices of criticism and debate would roar like never before if a station's shipment of singles from the record companies contained nothing of use to them. Here again we land on the question of use, a defining issue in contemporary Christian music.

Needs and Expectations

As long as I have been involved with contemporary Christian music, some in leadership have gently prodded artists and songwriters to focus their lyric writing on Jesus and on topics that are easily discerned as being related to Christianity. This approach has two sides, both of which must be taken into consideration. On one hand, it seems to demonstrate a genuine desire to communicate simply and clearly to the youngest and weakest of our brothers and sisters. This approach does not require that all people listen, think, and discern with the maturity that comes from having followed Jesus for many years. If this view is born out of genuinely wanting to love and serve people, and if at the same time there is also music for more mature, growing Christians, it is a good thing. On the other hand, intentions are not always so pure, and biblically informed thinking is not always the motivation.

Through the power of our positions and authority, many in CCM can influence lyrics in such a way that they mirror the felt needs and product expectations of Christian consumers. But when lyrics mirror these felt needs and product expectations without godly concern for whether they are healthy, legitimate, theologically sound, or complete, they cross a line into the shadows of the inauthentic life. Any movement away from the light of a scripturally informed, loving intent is a movement in the wrong direction.

Focusing the style or lyric content of music toward listeners is not wrong in and of itself. As I mentioned before, there are genuine reasons to do so—worship being chief among them. Consider another example: Christians need songs of celebration that mark important moments in their lives. In the context of a marriage ceremony, there is often a need for a beautiful song that speaks of marital love. If I write this type of song out of a love for the church, which is a natural extension of my love for God, then I am bearing fruit in keeping with one dimension or aspect of my calling as a musician and songwriter. In this scenario, I've done no harm in focusing both form and content in the direction of the consumers' need. However, if I create and promote music that seeks only to meet the Christian consumers' felt needs, to the exclusion of other needs that are equally important to the enrichment of their very human lives, I fall headlong into harm's way.

If my method for meeting the needs of God's people is to satisfy the need with the loudest voice, I can be assured that many important needs will go unmet. If I concentrate solely on one voice rather than the whole, if I concentrate only on the voices of humankind, I will never have a kingdom vision for music. It will forever elude me. It is one thing to possess a comprehensive kingdom vision for music and a genuine calli...

The focused, topical narrowness of CCM lyrics has its equivalent in the political arena. It reminds me of someone running for public office. If a Christian wants to win an election, for example, he or she tries to ensure that the maximum number of Christian voters go to the polls. He or she achieves this by focusing on the minimum number of issues that the maximum number of Christians will agree are most important. In the political arena, a comprehensive kingdom perspective is of little use in winning elections. It's too big, too vast, and too glorious. The very same scenario exists in CCM, except that in place of a cause, platform, or social issue is a lyrical emphasis. As with political issues, lyric ideas that produce a Christian consensus are very few. It seems that Christians gravitate toward subject matter out of an intuitive feeling that Christian music is at its most relevant when it's illuminating, propagating, and defending subject matter that is easily associated with the most basic Christian fundamentals.

Looking again to the political model, we should clearly see that Christianity is relevant to the abortion issue, for instance, and that the Christian mind ought to be brought to bear upon this important subject. Thinking again of CCM, we have no problem with the conviction that Jesus is relevant to Christian music. On the contrary, his relevance to Christian music could not be clearer. Yet a tension remains. If you write a song about DNA, how lovely your girlfriend is, or the call to care for the environment, it's likely you'll be thought of as someone who's failed to grasp the most basic concept behind the creation of a Christian lyric.

Those in the CCM community often assume that writers and artists who meet core consumer expectations for lyrics are "the ones who are serious about the Lord." Writers or artists who believe they have been called to a different mission and focus are apt to have their Christian commitment repeatedly called into question. In addition to potentially causing personal hurt to fellow human beings, accusations such as these go dangerously astray in their gross disregard for the sovereign purposes of God. They fail to take into account the doctrine of the body of Christ and the diversity and complexity of gifts, talents, callings, and responsibilities God gives to Christians for his countless and sovereign purposes. Furthermore, without what one artist called contemporary Christian music's "permanent Jesus stamp of approval,"[3] artists experience a difficult time of it, not only emotionally but financially as well. There are only so many spots for songs on the radio, and there are only so many people promoting concerts. Those without the stamp of approval are ushered to the back of the line or placed at the bottom of the list.

How Consumers Help Define What Is Christian

While many radio and retail gatekeepers hold strong convictions regarding the highest and best use of music, we cannot forget that the success of their own labor is directly tied to consumer and listener support. Their own survival requires them to listen and respond to the voices of those Christians who support their businesses and ministries. This reality cannot help but shape their notions of what a Christian lyric is—or isn't. Consumers of Christian music, whether they're tuning in to the radio, watching a video show, or purchasing a concert ticket or a CD, are voting on both the music and its lyrical content. By refusing to vote at the cash register (or with the dial or remote) for a particular song or artist when the lyric content fails to meet their criteria, they contribute to an industry-wide understanding of how Christian music is to be defined. Consumers hold fixed ideas about what they expect in music marketed as "Christian." For the most part, those

...ce responsibility. How well equipped are you as a follower of Jesus to discern whether lyrics are congruent with a comprehensive kingdom perspective, with the new way to be human that is found in Jesus? Everyone involved with Christian music, including the audience, is called to be interested in the same things Jesus is interested in. This is the kingdom. Certainly such a kingdom encompasses more than a set of easily identifiable terms common to Christianity.

From contemporary Christian music's position as an industry, the greatest argument for writing lyrics that improve listeners' ability to identify the music as Christian is that if they hear it and like it, they can find it again and support it in the marketplace. For example, listeners would know the music is "Christian" because they recognize words fundamental to Christianity. They would know whether the singer is male or female. They might even remember the song title or the lyrics from the chorus. All they would need to do is look for the music at a Christian bookstore, or in the Christian music section of a mainstream music retailer. The bottom line is this: Music that quickly and unmistakably identifies itself as Christian gets the consumer into the stores and in front of the product in the most cost-effective way. The benefits are real and substantial, both spiritually and economically. Sales activity in the stores produces revenue that pays for the cost of doing business. This translates into God's provision for many families. Profits are distributed to owners, investors, and shareholders. These monies are used to continue the capitalization and growth of all kinds of endeavors, including contemporary Christian music and local and global church ministries.

The spiritual benefits of steering Christians to musical product ought to be humbling and satisfying to those who create it, since God so often allows music and lyrics to touch lives in the simplest and grandest of ways. If people can do that with a few guaranteed Christian music buzzwords, it may be difficult for some to imagine there being any downside to it. But let's dig a little deeper.

DEPENDENT ON THE LYRIC

As I've pointed out, contemporary Christian music depends on the lyric to give listeners sufficient clues that they are indeed listening to Christian music and not any other genre of music. The decision to define and market Christian music as a genre based on the lyric has led to problems with serious consequences that serious followers of Jesus—who are called to live for God under his rule, everywhere and in everything—cannot ignore.

It's convenient for the CCM industry that their efforts to stimulate near-immediate product identification also serve traditional and legitimate ministry purposes. For example, some of the good purposes involve devotional, confessional, and worship themes. But because CCM uses the lyric and not the music to define its genre, and because of these legitimate ministry purposes, potential exists for the illegitimate use of legitimate lyrics. In short, some people eager for sales get excited when lyric content looks like healthy sales.

Anyone who writes songs of a worshipful, confessional, or devotional nature, or songs that directly proclaim the kingdom opportunity, uses language fundamental to Christianity. If the use of music is praise and worship, then naturally the music will incorporate language that articulates praise and worship of God. A lyric such as Charles Wesley's "O for a Thousand Tongues to Sing" is a good example of this, while my own "Monkeys at the Zoo" is not. Compare the two:

"O for a Thousand Tongues to Sing"

O for a thousand tongues to sing

My great Redeemer's praise,

The glories of my God and King,

The triumph...

...have been a whoring after things

'cause I want to feel safe inside, that's a big fat lie

No amount of green, gold, or silver

will ever take the place of the peace of God.[1]

Consider the language in each of these examples. Both of us were faithful to our intent, but look at the words Wesley used to articulate his intent: Redeemer, praise, glories, God, King, grace—all words commonly associated with Christianity. Now look at my lyric. You'll see that with the exception of "peace of God" at the end of the last line, I haven't used any language commonly associated with Christianity. Why? Is it because I don't know the first thing about writing a lyric congruent with following Jesus or with being interested in his agenda in the world? I hope not. My intent in writing the song was completely different from that of Wesley's. His lyric was directed to God, in praise of him. My lyric was directed at humankind in light of the reality of God. The intent gives shape to the outcome.

Since Wesley's commonly used "Christian" word count is so much higher than mine, his music naturally has a much greater chance of being identified as Christian music. If Wesley wrote his lyric as a praise response to God's grace, which I believe he did, then it's good he thought to choose language that simply, accurately, and poetically expressed his gratitude to God. We should all aspire to such a faithful response. For a moment, though, let's pretend that Wesley's intent was different from what history has recorded.

Reimagining Wesley for the Worse

Let's imagine that Wesley's use of words such as Redeemer, praise, glories, God, King, and grace were in fact intentional, but that his motive for using the words was something entirely different from framing a worshipful response to the gospel. Let's imagine that Wesley understood the church well enough to know that if he used "Christian" words in his songs, he could ensure a predictable outcome: (1) Even young, immature Christians would recognize and name "O for a Thousand Tongues" as Christian in origin, and (2) because of this recognition, Wesley's song would be accepted as relevant and useful to the Christian community. Let's also imagine Wesley understood that by creating the opportunity for the first predictable outcome, he would in turn create the possibility for the second outcome that might result in the sale of a copy of the music to "O for a Thousand Tongues."

Had Christian radio been around at the time of Charles Wesley, the Wesley I've conjured up in my imagination would know how to shape his lyrics for success. He would make these kinds of lyric choices to ensure that his song would meet the lyric criteria and expectations of Christian radio and its listeners. He would also have made these choices to ensure that youth pastors and various parachurch organizations would easily give his song their endorsement. He would have been compelled to pander to the keeper of any gate to which he desired entrance.

Because there are significant spiritual and economic benefits in steering listeners toward Christian music, it is often difficult for Christians to see the problems that have resulted from artists, industry, and audience working overtime to shape Christian music into a recognizable genre. The most significant problem is that these efforts make the gospel and the kingdom of God appear demonstrably different and tragically smaller than they actually are. We can get at the reason for this very quickly by analyzing the idea of genre and the bias it produces.

...ng forces are at work. While the idea of genre attempts to make the range of lyrical subject matter *smaller and less comprehensive* (more easily categorized and recognizable as "Christian"), the idea of what is truly Christian (as in "connected to the ways and agenda of Jesus") attempts to make lyrical content *bigger and more comprehensive*. In the latter, wider view, content becomes more difficult to recognize as truly Christian. Many Christians are likely to overlook indirect spiritual references, even when they are congruent with the all-encompassing narrative of the biblical Story or a general perspective of God's unfolding kingdom.

When we start talking about what defines lyric images and ideas as Christian, we have to recognize that Christian ideas are first and foremost kingdom ideas. Christians and Christianity sit inside something larger: the kingdom of God. The kingdom is a bigger idea than the church, even though the church is an incredibly important idea. The kingdom idea is far too big and important to fit within a genre. It's like trying to put the world's oceans in an eight-ounce glass. It can't be done; it's impossible. An eight-ounce glass could hold a drop or two from each ocean, but with its limited capacity, the glass could never pretend to contain all the oceans of the world. Likewise, no genre is big enough to hold a comprehensive kingdom perspective—it does not have the capacity. Genre is about reducing content. The kingdom is about expanding it. These two are incompatible. They just don't go together. They *can't* go together.

A comprehensive kingdom perspective sees the world as God sees it—or as much as is humanly possible. It seeks to see and act on the new kingdom opportunity for life that Jesus came to announce. At the heart of this perspective are two important truths:

1. Everything God created is good. He has called his people to be stewards of the good he created and to be his representatives in the kingdom at hand, everywhere and in everything. Therefore, everywhere and everything should be the subject matter of the lyrics Christians write. Christians should speak to what they know, and what they know should represent every aspect of creation. More than anything, lyrics should reflect what Jesus is interested in.

2. God has spoken in history. He has given his people a narrative that not only frames our view of what is real and lasting, but he reminds us that he acts in history on behalf of his people and that these acts are stories worthy of being told again and again. He is still acting on behalf of his people today, and we should be telling today's stories. All God's actions in history represent good and worthy subjects for lyrics written by followers of Jesus.

THE PEOPLE GET IT

The leadership of CCM has done a remarkable job of selling their music as a genre. People get it now. Television gets it—both late night and the morning shows. Magazines get it—even those not normally friendly to Christians, such as *SPIN*, *Details*, and *GQ*. Time-Life gets it. They're selling CCM on television just like they sell all the other genres. Everyone gets it. Unfortunately, what they get is usually a further reduction of our already reduced and marginalized version of Christianity and the kingdom of God. And it comes out so incredibly small that the result is like that eight-ounce glass trying to hold the oceans of the world. Only a few drops fit.

Here's an example of how one well-known sitcom got it: The March 19, 1998, episode of *Seinfeld* began with Elaine driving off in her boyfriend David Puddy's car. After pulling into traffic, she turned on the radio and began to bop along to the music. Suddenly ~~~~~~~~~~~~~~~~~~

Elaine quickly chose another preset station, only to find that her boyfriend had programmed every preset to a Christian radio station. Completely befuddled, Elaine muttered the word *Jesus,* only she wasn't recognizing the second person of the Trinity; she was taking the Lord's name in vain. Later, back at the restaurant, Elaine discussed the incident with George.

> *Elaine:* I borrowed Puddy's car, and all the presets on his radio were Christian rock stations.
>
> *George:* I like Christian rock. It's very positive. It's not like those real musicians who think they're so cool and hip.

Thank you, George, I'm sure Christian musicians everywhere will thank you for that. And "positive"—where have I heard that before? Didn't CCM have a try at Positive Country in the 1990s? Susie Luchsinger, Reba McIntire's sister, a singer who was marketed as Positive Country, never did agree with the tag. "What bothered me the most," says Susie, "is that when you say 'positive country,' well, then what's all the rest of it?… It's not all negative."[2]

According to former EMI Music president and CEO Jim Fifield, EMI got into the Christian music market because they "felt that the positive message that Christian artists convey would appeal to a much larger segment of the population."[3] Phil Quartararo, former president and CEO of Virgin Records America, told *CCM Magazine* that "there's no reason why we can't sell this to the mass appeal pop consumer, and it wouldn't hurt 'em to get a dose of a nice message."[4]

Positive and nice. Helpful and friendly. Hmm, sounds more like a description of the Ace Hardware man than music informed by a Story so huge it's still being written today—a Story so real that it involves every action, emotion, and thought under the sun; a complex, bloody, beautiful, redemptive, truthful Story. Positive and nice? Helpful and friendly? Certainly the martyr Stephen found his complete trust in Jesus helpful while he was being stoned to death by those who opposed his message. And I suppose you could say that he was nice or friendly to those who opposed him, since he cried out these words to Jesus right before he died: "Lord, do not hold this sin against them" (Acts 7:60). But is "nice" all we would say about his faith? Likewise, would we describe the crucifixion and resurrection of Jesus Christ with adjectives like these? As participants in the Story that God is telling on this earth, we should make and distribute music that elicits broader and deeper responses than "positive" and "nice."

It's Positively True

Many sincere Christians (you may find yourself among them) believe that Christianity is true because it works. They represent Christianity as if it were the best among today's glut of self-help programs and religions—a kind of higher form of self-help in which Jesus partners with the believer for the abundant life. But thinking of Christianity in this way and representing the kingdom of God as a self-help program is to totally misunderstand and misrepresent the Jesus way. The gospel or kingdom opportunity Jesus announced is not a self-help program that works; it is the truth about what is real. And because it is true and real, it possesses the power to change lives. Changed lives go on to change the world, and in this sense, Christianity does work, but not in the grossly limited ways in which people sometimes perceive it to work.

When we attempt to prove that the gospel is true because it is cool or positive, or because it renders unto us our version of the beautiful Christian life, we set the gospel—and Christianity as a whole—up for failure. This version of the gospel and the kingdom of God will eventually fail, because in reality it is no gospel and no kingdom at all. What many naive Western Christians do not understand is that there are places in the world where certain

...persisted in openly declaring the truthfulness of the Story and the falsehood of any religion or system of thought that contradicted it.

Contrary to what some earnest believers have stated, the problem with Christian lyrics isn't that not enough songs mention Jesus any more or that the "J" word is no longer hip. The problem is much bigger than the absence of Jesus's name in songs. The problem is that we've failed to hear and act on the calling to be God's people under his rule, everywhere and in everything. The problem is that we've failed to accurately represent the reality of what it means to follow Jesus and be serious about his creativity and agenda for life. This is the CCM problem.

The calling of the Christian music industry is to do the good it knows to do by composing true and beautiful music for the needs and purposes common to the gathering of the called ones—the church. Having shared in this privilege, people move outward into the "everywhere and everything." Here followers bring the comprehensive kingdom perspective to bear upon all of life. They ask a question such as, "What does God think about pain and suffering?" Then they study to know his thoughts and put those thoughts into the narrative of a song. They tell a story—an earthbound, kingdom-at-hand story, informed by the eternal God who possesses all knowledge and all truth. Followers keep alert and remain inquisitive. They ask another question and write another song. They do it again and again and again and never stop. That is why God's people, making God's music under his rule, legitimately touch on every aspect of God's dominion. And that is why this kind of music (whether or not you label it Christian) will never fit within a narrowly defined genre.

AN OCEAN OF POSSIBILITIES

Contemporary Christian music is a drop or two in the eight-ounce glass. A whole ocean of possibilities await the musical children of God, the men and women who equip them, all the people who listen now, and those who might listen in the future. The biblical Story tells us that through Jesus "all things were made" and that "without him nothing was made that has been made" (John 1:3).

How big is the kingdom? It's as big as Jesus imagined it to be. It is everywhere, and it is everything.

In the gospel of John, the author tells his readers that he transcribed not the whole story, but a true and sufficient story. According to John, "Jesus did many other things as well. If every one of them were written down, I suppose that even the whole world would not have room for the books that would be written" (John 21:25).

If there's not enough room in the gospel of John to tell the whole story of Jesus, there certainly isn't room within a rigidly defined musical genre to do the job. Before the contemporary Christian community can create, market, and support music that reflects the full impact and power of God's message to the church and the watching world, we have to stop making man-centered rules and guidelines for that message. We're in no position to define God's boundaries. We can't put the ocean in a glass. We can't stuff music created by Christians into a genre.

As John noted in his gospel, Jesus's interests and concerns touched on every facet of human experience. If Jesus were to appear to you in the quiet of your home, have a seat at your table, and explain to you in scientific, new-physics detail how he's the glue that holds all things together in the universe, would you wonder to yourself, *What's "Christian" about what he's telling me?*

It's a silly question, but no sillier than ~~~~~~~~~~~~~~~~~~~~~~~~~~~~

~~~~~~~~~~~~~~~ any enterprise is controlled by the sound of the cash register and the applause of people, the more the audience response matters. But what really matters most?

Look at the ocean of God's music all around you. Imagine with me, and throw away that glass.

n some corners of the CCM community, there is a sense that continuing to pursue a reasonable consensus on the role of the lyric is, well, unreasonable. Many people—artists, industry folk, and audience—have long since gone on to construct various rationalizations to explain their choices and to deal with the tension and confusion that surround the subject.

They bring these feelings of "enough already" to their roles as creators and marketers. They understand that consumers won't take the time to read or to think things through because they don't have the time or the inclination to do so. The result is that the contemporary use of language in all its forms, from lyrics to advertising copy, is limited to the superficial. Everything is made small. Industry insiders know that the Christian music audience does not often stop to think about whether a lyric is harmonious with a biblical worldview or a comprehensive kingdom perspective, because they themselves so often do not. Instead, people tend to filter lyrics through a mental grid with chicken-wire openings, rather than listening through a more discerning grid with window-screen openings. Information deserving attention, both contrary to and congruent with the controlling Story, slips through unnoticed. This information flows through without recognition, not because it is less important, but because it is made to *seem* less important or irrelevant in relationship to the things Christian culture views as important and relevant.

Following the Wrong Leader

More often than not, the contemporary Christian music industry shapes its lyric content to follow the lead of those in the Christian music audience (the church) who are the least inclined to think Christianly about broader life issues. Songwriters and artists admit doing it, and publishers and record-company leaders admit encouraging it. Most of the industry understands this to be one of the limitations of writing for the church and accepts it as such. Though there are notable exceptions, most of the time the industry considers this state of affairs to be rigidly unchangeable, and this is where it errs.

It is wrong for leaders in the contemporary Christian music industry, when writing lyrics for the Christian marketplace, to give in to the church's general unwillingness to think on or cultivate a kingdom perspective. What is most disturbing is that rather than seeing the church's inability to discern spir-itually and think Christianly as a cause for tears, people view these enormously important issues as everyday problems for which pragmatic solutions must be found. They diligently work toward answers that will help them not only carry out the day-to-day business of Christian music but achieve success as the world and the forces of capitalism view it. CCM insiders often appear to be more concerned with this particular mission than with the mission of tending to the overall spiritual health of the body of Christ—of doing good to every-one, especially believers (see Galatians 6:10).

Rather than living in response to grace and in the knowledge of the king-dom of God, many in CCM react to the consumer alone and let the market-place define how they think, create, perform, and subsequently live. This is incongruent with our primary calling to live as God's people under his rule. Followers of Jesus are not to be defined or ruled by anything other than God's will and way. It is his lead we are to follow.

The church's general inability to discern spiritually, think Christianly, and demonstrate a comprehensive kingdom perspective is a serious health problem in the body of Christ. These issues ought to inspire our imaginations to create music that addresses them—music that models a comprehensive perspective on life and initiates good thinking, good imagining, prayer

...... .u. ..ic uissemination of ideas. Nor is it something God created as a kind of sleight of hand to get otherwise disinterested humans interested in important ideas. On the contrary, music, like language, is an integral part of God's creation. He has built into both an intrinsic power and benefit that we must respect. When the two are brought together in the form of vocal music, there are consequences. If the creator of the vocal music has respected both the music and the language, there is great potential for both music and language to shine brighter together than if they are heard separately. In order to achieve this, the two must become one in such a way as to yield to each other without becoming less than what they were created to be. The marriage of music and lyric is very much like a human marriage in this respect.

For this reason, I maintain that unless listeners can appreciate the music on some level, be it the melody, rhythm, style, production, or emotional response, they will receive little perceivable benefit from an easily recognizable Christian lyric. Unless listeners like something about the music, apart from the lyric, it is unlikely they will engage the lyric on any level other than the superficial. Please understand that I believe God can do anything he wants with human effort, be it extraordinary or ridiculous. Yet just because God is in control, it does not mean that his people are exempt from thinking things through. Nevertheless, I understand this to be an arguable point, since many

Christians believe that one of the strongest reasons to advocate lyrics that are easily recognizable as Christian in origin is that they disseminate the Word of God, and the Word of God shall not return void.

The idea that God's Word does not return void appears in the book of Isaiah:

For as the rain comes down, and the snow from heaven,

And do not return there,

But water the earth,

And make it bring forth and bud,

That it may give seed to the sower

And bread to the eater,

So shall My word be that goes forth from My mouth;

It shall not return to Me void,

But it shall accomplish what I please,

And it shall prosper in the thing for which I sent it. (55:10-11, NKJV)

In context, the thirteen verses in Isaiah 55 frame an invitation to the nation of Israel to take hold of the life that is truly life. The chapter begins with a call for Israel to come to the One who alone can meet Israel's truest needs. Next comes the promise of an everlasting covenant (one eventually fulfilled in Christ and his church). Then comes a call to repentance. And finally, renewal, the lifting of the curse and the forgiveness of sin.

According to scholar Alec Motyer, who has devoted most of his life to the study of Isaiah, the central preoccupation of this chapter "is with the Word of the Lord," and the "Word" in question is "directly the Word of the Lord."[1] As the Scripture emphatically states, it is God's Word going forth from God's mouth that makes good the guarantee that God's Word will not return to him void. The emphasis here is on God and the power of his direct Word to create and effect change.

Belief in the power of God's direct Word as Creator and Redeemer, the One who can create and effect change, is a belief absolutely central to Christianity. However, if we emphatically state that a four-minute "Christian" pop song carries this same identical weight and effect... ...intended but nevertheless human and fallible thoughts and purposes.

In his commentary on Isaiah, Motyer writes, "The Word of God is the unfailing agent of the will of God." Motyer reminds us of the deep connection between God's Word and God's will. We cannot divorce the Word of God from his will. His Word accomplishes what he has willed it to accomplish. This is why his Word does not return to him void. Motyer continues, "As the rain furnishes both seed and bread, so the word of God plants the seed of repentance in the heart and feeds the returning sinner with the blessed consequences repentance produces." It is by the power of his Word that God "wills and effectuates the repentance that brings sinners home to himself."[2]

With the best of intentions and the worst of methods, artists, industry people, and CCM fans have distorted the meaning of these Scriptures, perpetuating a false view of them year after year. Christians have been, to borrow a phrase from noted author Richard Weaver, "hysterically optimistic" regarding the power of CCM. In theory, people may believe that the emphasis of Isaiah 55:11 is on God and the power of his direct Word to create and effect change, but in practice they turn it around. They act as if it is God's Word going forth from humanity's mouth that makes good the guarantee that God's Word will not return to humanity void. In acting this way, they place the emphasis on the human ability to use the power of God's Word—and various lyrical derivations of it—to create and effect change for the desire and will of humankind in God's name. This is not what these Scriptures teach. Everyone who takes the Word seriously must be careful not to turn the good Word of God into a kind of lucky charm that is rubbed into songs to justify having created them.

Does God ever use four-minute "Christian" pop songs laced with Scripture and spiritual principles as an example of his Word not returning void? I imagine so, but only if it's his will. Remember, Satan quoted Scripture to Jesus, but it didn't inspire Jesus to change his mind (see Luke 4:9-12).

I believe that one of the reasons the Christian music community has embraced this idea and perpetuated it for so long is that it provides a seemingly critique-proof justification for many of its choices regarding music and lyric. How can critics inside and outside the church possibly find anything wrong with music that carries the power of the direct Word of God?

REACTING TO THE CONTENT

When the church gathers to worship God in his majesty, the language of the lyric must reflect the intent and purposes of worship. It must of necessity use words common to its purpose, common to known translations of the Story.

There are many benefits to creating lyrics that are clearly Christian. Some Christian listeners will respond to the music sooner and may enjoy it more. Once they realize the lyric is Christian, they can confidently enter into the music. Serving the listeners' comfort level is a benefit as well. Some listeners are uncomfortable with anything other than Christian music. They listen exclusively to Christian music out of a perceived obedience to God (and as a matter of conscience). These brothers and sisters are only comfortable when they can listen to music with the assurance that they're not violating their conscience. Familiar words common to Christianity help assure these listeners that they're giving their hearts and minds to something they believe to be appropriate and safe.

When non-Christian listeners hear Christian music, the fact that they are able to easily recognize the music as "Christian" improves the possibility of a response to the content. The response may be:

1. Positive—the listener is open, and remain~~~~~~~~~~~~~~~~~~~~~~~~~~~~

~~~~~~~~~~~~~~~~~~~~ ~~~~ bought the CD."

This example helps people see how creating songs that are easily recognizable as Christian in origin might in fact be a good thing.

2. Negative—the listener is closed, and remains closed, to easily recognizable Christian content regardless of whether he or she perceives the music as good. For example: "I really liked the song and wasn't too far into it when I realized, hey, this is a Christian song, which really bummed me out because I was really liking the song a lot. The music was cool, but the lyrics just don't relate to my life. It's not what I'm into spiritually at all and especially not politically. There's so much that's political about the Christian Right that I just don't agree with, and truthfully it just turns me off to the whole thing."

This example helps people see how creating songs that are easily recognizable as Christian in origin might in fact be counterproductive, especially when common words, phrases, or clichés trigger negative associations and comparisons. Here, common words, phrases, and clichés actually distract from the very truths they seek to communicate. The listener doesn't think about what the artist is saying in the lyrics. The listener believes he knows what a Christian is and what Christians are about and wants nothing to do with them or their music. Scott and Chris Dente from Out of the Grey anticipated this kind of reaction when they first started writing songs: "Our initial approach to songwriting was based on the idea that you don't hit people with a sledgehammer, because they put their religious God-filters up when they hear certain phrases and words."[3]

3. *Indifferent*—the listener remains largely ambivalent to easily recognizable Christian content, regardless of whether he or she perceives the music as good, bad, or somewhere in between. This kind of reaction is common to listeners who are committed relativists and/or pluralists. For example: "I really liked the song and wasn't too far into it when I realized, hey, this is a Christian song. So what, though, everybody's entitled to their own spirituality as long as it's positive. It's a good song—not so incredibly good that I have to run right out and buy it, but if somebody gave me a copy, I'd probably listen to it."

This example helps people see how our pluralistic culture has allowed Christianity to occupy a spot on the menu of spiritualities available to the religious consumer. In this case, the use of clichés and common Christian terms so easily identifies the work as being "Christian" that even though it's recognized as Christian in origin, it is not engaged intellectually on any level. It is acknowledged and tolerated, but not necessarily taken seriously, especially as a declaration of what is real for all people at all times.

Wait Till You See the Side Effects

Serving the Christian listener's comfort level has an unfortunate side effect: It often works against the spiritual maturity and growth of the church. This is because many immature Christians live radically compartmentalized lives and, as a result, arrange their music purchasing and listening into compartments as well—compartments that correspond to their felt needs.

For example, if this type of listeners need to feel romantic, they might listen to the love songs of Usher or Luther Vandross on their local radio station. Or they might purchase romantic music at their local mainstream music retailer. On the other hand, if they need to feel "Christian," they might listen to Christian music on their local Christian radio station. Or they might pur-

chase Christian music at their local Christian music retailer. They do not turn
to mainstream love songs to feel hopeful and heaven bound. Nor do they often
turn to Christian music to feel romantic or to have God's thoughts about love
and romance enter into their own. This type of Ch~~ristian li~~

~~which self is the arbiter of life, is self-destructive."[4]~~

These consumers know what they want and are uncomfortable and disappointed with music that declares itself to be Christian (either directly or
indirectly), yet does not meet their personal religious needs. For them the ability to easily identify the music as "Christian" or to have record companies or
retailers give it their "permanent Jesus stamp of approval" takes the guesswork
out of shopping and ensures that they will indeed purchase only the kind of
product they want.

A retail advisor to EMI CMG posed this question several years ago:
"What is a Christian album?" The answer, he suggested, is up to the consumer.
"Why do people shop Christian music and bookstores?" he continued. "I
believe it is summed up in the orthodoxy. In today's economy, Christians will
buy their Kenny G, Garth Brooks, Frank Sinatra, and Counting Crows at just
about any place, fully expecting that it will possibly/probably not be an album
of Christian values. But when it comes time to buy an album for their
friend/relative/selves, they want quality control of sorts. What will this album
say? Will it have the substance that I am shopping for? When it comes to lyrical content," he concluded, "most music buyers…rely on the record companies to police the content of their albums until somebody complains at the
consumer level."[5]

Most record companies understand their role in policing the content. In

1998 I surveyed thirty-five popular CCM artists and groups, and 37 percent of those polled answered yes to the question, "Has a Christian publisher or record-label executive ever asked or required you to change a lyric because, in his or her opinion, the lyric was theologically or biblically incorrect?"

Twenty-five percent also answered yes to the question, "Has a Christian publisher or record-label representative ever asked or required you to add a name for God, such as Jesus, Father, Spirit, or Lord to the lyric of a song?" One artist who answered no added, "They roll out the red carpet when you do."

Rather than seeing the psychological hedonism Wells described as a problem to grieve over and pray about, many industry insiders see this kind of thinking and behavior as indicative of consumer trends that must be followed and served for the industry to stay profitable. Even Christians, it seems, must live by the motto "The customer is always right." It sounds charitable enough and superficially smart from a business standpoint, but it's really more Dale Carnegie than Jesus in origin. Since Christians are supposedly student-followers of Jesus, we have other issues to factor in—especially those of us involved in books and music.

In an e-mail sent to EMI CMG, the retail advisor mentioned above proposed this question to a colleague of mine: "As a Christian concerned about content, isn't it my responsibility to honor my customers' trust?"

To this question I would reply, "Don't we have a responsibility to God, his church, and his kingdom to create, manufacture, and stock on store shelves books and music that tell the whole kingdom story to date—a unified, yet diversified story? Aren't Christians called to see things as God sees them, that is, as much as humanly possible? Isn't this the Christian maturity Paul advocates?"

The church and the watching world deserve artists, songwriters, and businesspeople who prayerfully seek inspiration and wisdom to create and market music that is truly good—music that meets a great number of legitimate needs. But to get this, consumers must be diligent, and they must not allow the industry to treat them merely as retail-sales targets. Because consumers are image-bearing people first and consumers second, those of us who are creators, marketers, and retailers must want what is good for people over and above what we know we can sell them. The responsibility goes both ways.

This is a Christian approach to creativity

I n September 1997 I was asked by the Awards and Criteria Committee of the Gospel Music Association Board of Directors to join an advisory group formed to help the GMA produce "a succinct, working definition of what constitutes 'Gospel Music.' "[1] At that time the committee was in the process of revisiting the "criteria upon which recorded product is eligible to be nominated for, and receive, a Dove Award."[2] According to the letter they sent me, this revisiting of the criteria had come about because some Christian Booksellers Association member stores were stocking recorded music not "Christian" in nature.

After three days of trying hard to contribute something, I concluded that coming up with a definition was both too simple and too complex. To say that "gospel music" is music that communicates the good news of Jesus Christ's atonement for sin is simple and true, and this in fact might be one definition. But sticking to this kind of succinct definition left me troubled. Under a definition this narrow, the majority of songs I had contributed to contemporary Christian and pop music over the previous sixteen years could not be categorized as gospel music. This kept me searching for answers.

What I now know for certain is this: Jesus Christ and the good news of the gospel defines life as I know it. For more than twenty years now, the new kingdom opportunity has inspired and informed my life. Everything I believe about anything is either informed by or checked by the controlling Story known as the Bible. I received the Bible as God's word to me after having believed the good news story of Jesus. My life and my work move outward from the life and teachings of Messiah Jesus, the gospel or good-news story-teller. This, however, is where the complexity really begins. From this point outward, trying to define gospel music is a bit like trying to lasso DNA. It is simple to say that gospel music is either music about the gospel of Jesus Christ or music in praise of Jesus, the source of the gospel. It is another thing altogether to attempt to extract a sound-bite definition of gospel music from what it means to live in light of the Jesus story about the new kingdom opportunity and the forgiveness of sin that traveled along with it.

Stumped, I wrote back to the GMA stating that "I regret that I cannot provide you with a definition that honors both the simplicity and complexity of the gospel, takes into account the seriousness of the gospel, and gives you and your committee a definition for the purpose of identifying music which does or does not qualify for a Dove Award."

Many questions remained. Among them: What does it mean for a created thing to be Christian in nature? Can a created thing actually and truly be Christian in nature? And what are the ramifications of naming created things "Christian"?

What's in a Name?

The act of naming is an essential part of our stewardship role in creation. Names are derived from the distinctiveness of the thing being named. Though human beings are distinct in that we alone know the privilege of bearing God's image, we were not created as distinctly "Christian" in the sense that we understand this term to mean a student-follower of Messiah Jesus. We must become a disciple of Jesus Christ in order to be called a Christian. Even then our distinctiveness is extrinsic in that it's imparted to us by Christ at our new birth into the new way. Christians are named after Christ, to whom we belong. Furthermore, this Christian distinctiveness is at first an inward reality, which over time (hours, days, and years) manifests itself outwardly, in ways of being human unique to those who are the called-out-ones. God's

_____ beings are offered God's plan of reconciliation by grace through faith in Jesus Christ. Only human beings can mirror God's image. Only human beings can follow Jesus as his disciples, carrying out the image-bearing activity of being God's direct representatives on earth in the kingdom at hand in the name of Jesus, under the guidance of the Holy Spirit, for God's purposes, and to his Glory, everywhere and in everything.

If this is all true, then it would appear that all the things people so easily name as "Christian," such as Christian music, Christian coffeehouses, Christian motorcycle clubs, and Christian radio, do not possess the *creational integrity* to be called Christian in a biblical sense. "Creational integrity" is just another way of saying that something is true to the way it was created. Consider a chair. It is a human creation. There are ideas integral to a chair. A chair has a creational integrity quite different from a created animal such as the giraffe. Because of this, you would not mistakenly identify a giraffe as a chair. We know to name these created things in keeping with what they actually are. If there are ideas integral to what it means for a human to be Christian and it is impossible for other created things to possess them, you can see how naming things like music "Christian" would be problematic.

However, one can make a case for naming things "Christian" because they have a Christian beginning, in that Christians provide the economic support for them to exist, with an end goal in mind somehow connected to ideas fundamental to Christianity, such as contemporary Christian music. Or you might make a case for calling things "gospel" in order to indicate that it is for the purposes, wants, and needs of Christians who believe in the gospel that these types of things—such as the Gospel Music Association—exist. There is no crime in having organizations, events, and various other entities (such as the Democratic National Convention or Alcoholics Anonymous) named so that they directly reflect the thinking or identity of their participants. One is for Democrats; the other for alcoholics. If Democrats are planning their national convention and hope other Democrats will attend, it would be prudent to refer to the event as the Democratic National Convention. Likewise, if you are a recovering alcoholic traveling through a city on business and would like to attend an AA meeting, it would be helpful to be able to open the phone book and look up Alcoholics Anonymous. If you are creating, marketing, and selling products you believe only Christians will be interested in (for the most part), then it may be prudent to put the word "Christian" in the name of your business. For some this is just common sense. But it is not a neutral choice. All ideas have consequences, including the idea of naming things "Christian."

THE REALITY OF KINGDOM LIFE

There are at least two problems associated with naming things "Christian." As we discussed earlier, we first have to recognize that Christian ideas and things are kingdom ideas and things *before* they are Christian. Christians and Christianity sit inside something larger—the kingdom of God. People are certainly free to speak of something Jesus taught his disciples as a "Christian" idea. But, truthfully, if it is a Christian idea, it is part of a much larger gathering of ideas—kingdom ideas. Even more specifically, these ideas given to the world by Jesus are kingdom ideas about what constitutes reality, about what it means to be truly human. Because it's a kingdom agenda that Jesus came announcing, not a Christian one, the kingdom of God trumps Christian culture. Don't give up on this. It may take some time to understand.

For example, Christians would consider the Lord's Supper a Christian idea or concept, and if you were to write a song ab~~~ ~~~ ~~~~~~~~~~

~~~~~~~~~~~~~~~~~~~~~~~ ~~~~~~~~ ~~ redemption. Kingdom life is life that is abundant and full to overflowing. This is what we want to be about. You can't reduce this. It's too big to wrap your arms around it. Too big for any convenient label.

Small privatized ideas about Jesus as the personal Savior can be reduced to fit inside a half-hour sitcom. What we want to be about is something that is so enormous, so life-penetrating, that it cannot be contained in all the sitcoms in the world. Songs informed by a comprehensive kingdom perspective will not be small. They will include all of history as well as visions for the future.

When the reality of kingdom life is defined in small, restrictive terms, Christians begin to think that those terms represent the kingdom. It is not uncommon for songwriters to perpetuate a truncated kingdom view in their lyrics. And it's out of this small, insufficient picture of the reality of kingdom life that Christian music gets categorized, the good news of Jesus gets trivialized, and authentic faith in him gets caricatured. Ironically, many songwriters who do not profess a relationship with God write truthful songs that cast a huge vision of life. This ought to shame Christians who say they know God but fail to address the whole of his earthly interests.

In order to connect with the agenda of God in the world, the Christian music community must begin to write music and lyric from a kingdom perspective, regardless of the pulse of the consumer or the official definitions of "gospel" or "Christian" music. Psalm 19:1 says, "The heavens declare the glory of God; the skies proclaim the work of his hands." Granted, it wouldn't represent the most commercially viable of topics, and I understand that it might render me ineligible for a Dove Award, but I'd be willing to write, record, and market a song about the relationship between quantum mechanics and the glory of God.

When Christians name media, vocational pursuits, inanimate objects, and all their various activities as "Christian," they must remember an important fact: The thing being named was not empty of meaning and purpose prior to their naming of it. It was not a neutral entity waiting to be Christianized. It has its own unique design or creational integrity; it also has its own ideological bias.

If people could name things "Christian" and allow them to keep their creational integrity, there would be little reason to examine the issue. Unfortunately, it can't be done. For example, consider a Christian coffeehouse. Before a coffeehouse ever becomes "Christian," it is first a place where, we hope, excellent coffee is served at a fair market price to people who find pleasure in drinking coffee. A coffeehouse may do other things like serve food and provide a forum for musical performers and poets, but a coffeehouse is only a coffeehouse to the degree that it possesses the creational integrity of one. A little storytelling will cement this point.

A Cup of Good Coffee

In college Tom Watson had been a strong student leader active in the Fellowship of Christian Athletes. Upon graduation Tom and two close friends, Jake and Eric, decided to pool their life savings into opening a Christian coffeehouse on the main street of Blakeford, their little college town. They rented a storefront and set about the task of turning it into what Jake referred to as "a place cool enough for nonbelievers to hang out at." Jake wasn't joking with this comment. All three were in it for the ministry, not out of a burning love for coffee. They were on fire for Jesus, and more than anything, they wanted people to become Christians as a result of their efforts. Not that they didn't want to do good business; they did. In fact, together they had pledged to always pay their bills on time and to be extra courteous to all their customers, since they wouldn't necessarily know if a customer was Christian

...houses along Telegraph Avenue. So it was with some interest that he read the flyer he'd plucked from beneath the left windshield wiper of his Volvo that announced, "Killer coffee and killer sounds! / All in a cool Christian atmosphere."

"So, the Christians have opened themselves a coffeehouse," he mumbled under his breath. He smiled and grunted, "I wonder if an old Jew can breathe in a Christian atmosphere?"

It was just before five o'clock on Friday when Professor Kahane walked through the door of Mars Hill Coffee. He found a seat on a comfortable couch across from two students he recognized from State.

"Good afternoon," he said to them in his best professorial voice as he reached out to retrieve a large book from the coffee table. It was titled *Jack,* a biography of C. S. Lewis. The professor had always appreciated Lewis. Of course he didn't agree with Lewis's theological conclusions, but he admired him as a writer and a thinker. He placed the book down and took a sip of his coffee. Lukewarm.

What is this? He wondered. *It's definitely not the dark roast of my experience.* Disappointed, the professor put down the cup. He had so wanted it to be good. He really had hoped to recommend the place to friends and faculty members. Blakeford needed a coffeehouse, and he'd hoped this would be it. He pledged to himself to come back; they deserved the chance to improve. On the way out he caught the eye of a young man folding and counting T-shirts—shirts presumably for sale. The young man was modeling his fare. Emblazoned on the front of the shirt: "This Blood's for You."

Not for me, thought the prof. *How do they take any of this seriously—something trivialized to this degree and handled with so little reverence?*

Six weeks later, Tom, Jake, and Eric received a kind letter from Professor Kahane on his personal letterhead that together they read aloud with great anticipation.

Dear friends at Mars Hill,

Six weeks ago I was delighted to hear of the news of your opening. I've thought for a long time that we've needed a good coffeehouse in Blakeford. Unfortunately, after trying your establishment several times, it is my opinion that you've shot a bit wide of good, and need improvement in several areas. The first and most important area that needs improvement is the basic cup of coffee you serve. Frankly, it is not good coffee. Have you folks been to very many coffeehouses? Something tells me you haven't. Who is your coffee vendor? Are they reputable?

It may or may not matter to you in the big picture, but I won't be coming back, at least not for a while. After some time has passed, if you are still open for business, I will return to try your coffee again. Please tell the thin blond girl with the nose ring that, no, I still do not want to receive Jesus Christ as my personal savior. All I want right now is a good cup of coffee.

Respectfully,

Professor Kahane

Tom put down the letter and sunk into the nearest chair. Jake did as well. Eric was not so passive: "Man, I told you guys we should never have bought those cheap beans."

The Naming and the Damage Done

I've led you on this fictional journey in hopes of making a point: Naming something "Christian" is not a neutral choice. It's a choice that must be carefully and prayerfully thought out. Christians ought to

[text obscured]

...should be known for serving the best coffee in town at a great price, not for having "Christian" on their sign in the parking lot. In this way, the Christians' vocation honors the call to live good lives in view of their community. You do not have to name a coffeehouse "Christian" to justify owning one. Neither do you have to have some other primary motivation for getting into the coffee business, such as evangelism. To think this way is to have a very odd view of what it means to evangelize—to tell the Story of God, people, and place through word and work.

The "Christian" name tag becomes an easy target when things go wrong. When a "Christian" business fails to honor its commitments, it drags the name of Jesus down with it in the eyes of people outside the Christian community. Our Professor Kahane was a fictional example, but I have seen far too many real ones among the recording studio managers, musicians, and engineers in Nashville. As a record producer I work closely with these people, and for years I've heard their horror stories of not being paid on time by "Christian" music businesses, being nickeled and dimed to death by them for lower fees, and so on. Because these people identify themselves as Christians, their violation of the integrity of the music business (bad enough) is transformed into a violation of the integrity of their faith story before the watching world (far worse). Better that colleagues and customers know Christians by their love and good deeds than by their letterhead or neon sign.

When my son Sam was a little boy, he asked me to take him to the store to buy some Coke. In his estimation our family needed to start drinking a whole lot more of it. When we asked why, Sam replied with a perfectly straight face, "So we can recycle."

Anytime we set something up as a front for something else, things get silly. And more often than not, people can see right through the facade.

Perhaps the single greatest problem with naming anything "Christian" (apart from the church and things directly related to it) is that in doing so people always seem to end up misrepresenting God and the good way of life modeled by Jesus. God cannot be contained in things made by the hands of fallen humanity. The church is the only thing he has given his name to, and perhaps it should remain that way.

"Christian" Confusion

It is unfortunate that the industry has successfully established CCM as a competitive genre. This works against Christians who try to place artists from the Christian music community in the mainstream. And the issue seldom gets down to resistance based on the truth claims of Jesus Christ. The opposition is more often framed this way: "If you're a 'Christian' act, what are you doing trying to make a go of it in the pop arena? You have your own genre to work in."

The Christian music industry has taught the world that the music is Christian without teaching them what "Christian" actually means. As a result, people have come to believe that Christian music is a genre like jazz or Latin music. When those with a comprehensive view of music take an artist from the Christian community (who wears the tag "Christian artist") and equip him or her to be a competitive artist in the culture at large (rather than in the church), this is often very confusing to the pop music infrastructure and its gatekeepers. In this scenario, naming the artist "Christian" undermines the musical/artful mission rather than clarifying and supporting it.

There are at least three excellent reasons why Christians should stop naming everything Christian:

1. Christians could no longer choose to purchase things simply because they were "Christian." They would be forced to decide ~~~~~~ ...ings. They would be forced out into the everywhere and everything of the kingdom at hand. As a result, they would be more faithful to the Christian mission, and they would come closer to being God's people, in God's place, under God's rule.

3. Non-Christians could no longer write off Christians and their work without encountering them directly. Non-Christians would have to deal honestly with Christians, their work, and their ideas. Honesty, integrity, and charity would be wonderful things to recover. Direct interaction would foster real dialogue, not the nasty habit of writing people off with convenient labels.

When I imagine such scenarios, I start to see more ocean than drops in the glass. Yet, I know that when people start to imagine, talk, and write in the way I've been doing for the last little bit, there is great potential to be misunderstood. Please understand that I have a high view of the calling to create good and truthful music for the church in a number of settings for a number of purposes. Don't interpret my willingness to write songs about quantum mechanics as promoting a new lyric direction for contemporary Christian music. All I'm concerned about promoting is the Jesus way of being human, his kingdom, and faithfulness to what he's called his people to. Since I'm a musician, I'm concerned with how this plays out for musicians.

Also, please don't hear in my "three excellent reasons" to stop naming everything Christian a demand that people cease and desist immediately with calling themselves Christian. What I'm concerned about here at the crossroads is doing the difficult work of carefully thinking through these issues in order to discern which way is forward. Those who take this discussion seriously will have to decide for themselves which direction that is. For myself, I'm praying to remain a teachable sinner—someone more afraid of not knowing the truth than of having been found in error. And so I'm fearfully wrestling, looking for the way that reflects what Jesus is interested in.

Two Views

The debate over lyric content is between two main groups. The first group represents those who believe Christian music should be "Christian." They think that, with few exceptions, Christian music should exist to represent lyrical themes related to CCM's original mission of worship and evangelism. Some in this group have imitated and championed the "lyric criteria" we discussed earlier. Some endorse a sacred/secular split. Still others maintain that lyrics should adhere to common Christian lyrical themes in order to be named and marketed as "Christian." Without the "Christian" name tag, some would not oppose a greater diversity of subject matter for lyrics written by Christians. They just don't want it to be called "Christian."

The second group represents those Christians who believe music created by Christians ought to promote lyrics that reflect a comprehensive Christian worldview, which is nearly the same as what I've been calling a comprehensive kingdom perspective. In short, this group believes that everything under God's view and care is worthy subject matter for songwriting.

As heated as the debate has become at times, I still maintain that these two groups are not as polarized as they might think. For example, to promote lyrics that reflect a comprehensive Christian worldview or kingdom perspective is to promote worship and evangelism (telling the Story). In this way, the kingdom-perspective group does support the agenda of the worship and evangelism group—in principle if not always in practice. Where the second group differs from the first group is in their promotion of thinking Christianly about all of life and in the belief that all of life can and should be

...from Scripture, which is comprised of stories, sermons, genealogies, prayers, letters, songs, poems, and proverbs of every conceivable style and incorporates every imaginable literary device from hyperbole to alliteration to acrostic to stream of consciousness. The subject matter is all of life, both the hellish and the heavenly.

The same Scripture that brings us the good news of Jesus Christ also tells the story of a fat king named Eglon, who was murdered by a left-handed man named Ehud. When Ehud stabbed the fat king, Scripture says that, "Ehud did not pull the sword out, and the fat closed in over it" (Judges 3:22). The Scripture is chock-full of this kind of truthful, descriptive narrative.

The same Scripture that describes the ministry of the Holy Spirit also includes these words: "Let him kiss me with the kisses of his mouth—for your love is more delightful than wine" (Song of Songs 1:2).

These remarkable passages were included in God's Word for a reason. Yet if stories or phrases like these were shaped into songs and recorded by Christian artists, it's likely that many well-meaning people would insist that there is simply no place in Christian music for songs about the murder of portly kings and lovemaking "more delightful than wine." The Christian worldview/kingdom perspective group is asking for the freedom to shine the light of Christ and his Word on myriad subjects (though we hope not portly kings).

The first, or "lyric criteria," group is calling for faithfulness in singing about the Christian understanding of God, faithfulness in honoring him in worship, and faithfulness in spreading the message of the gospel (or good news of the kingdom). If you are a Christian, you must share this group's concern. If you are in the second group, I appeal to you to communicate to those in the first group that you believe Christians ought to be about communicating the gospel, living lives of worship, and bringing the truth of Scripture to bear on a multitude of topics. Tell them you want to make the invisible kingdom visible.

BOLSTERING THE BIG IDEA

It's hard for me to imagine that the group championing lyric criteria really believes that Christian artists ought to abandon commentary on culture or avoid addressing the most basic of human concerns in lyrics. To believe in such a way would be especially difficult for parents. While you might teach your child about the lordship of Messiah Jesus over all of life, he or she would soon learn that Christian music has very little to do with the lordship of Christ over all of life. And if your child wanted to listen to music having to do with love or romance or a host of other topics, he or she would have to turn somewhere other than music created by followers of Jesus. This doesn't square.

I understand the zeal of the worship-and-evangelism group to promote Jesus and the gospel. I would hope everyone involved in this often fiery debate shares this passion. But I must give a firm but gentle warning: By enforcing lyric criteria, you are lowering the bar, not raising it. You're making it far too easy to enter your gates. You are unknowingly creating a climate where it is fast becoming more admirable and profitable for artists to *appear* Christian in the most simple and superficial sense than to *be* Christian in the most biblically comprehensive sense. As a result, striking a rock-star pose and hoarsely commanding the audience to spell out J-E-S-U-S is often interpreted as an unwavering commitment to Christ, whereas lyrically addressing all of life through a comprehensive kingdom perspective is often misinterpreted as lacking commitment to Christ. This should not be. If you are serious about the Jesus way, you ought to be asking how this could be. Next, start doing something to turn this error around.

God has called his people to something profound.

...need to do it soon, before we thoroughly confuse not only our own children but the talented and gifted artists coming up who want nothing more than to live out the reality of kingdom life everywhere and in everything.

To my readers who represent CCM's listeners and supporters, I ask that you contribute your part in raising the bar of the CCM industry. Consider whether you yourself have played a role in creating a climate where it's more admirable and financially profitable for Christian artists to *appear* Christian in a superficial sense than to *be* Christian in the most biblically comprehensive sense. Are you looking for easily recognizable words common to Christians in the lyrics of Christian artists? Or are you looking and listening for great music written from a comprehensive kingdom perspective—music that might touch you, challenge you, and bring you pleasure in a multitude of ways, including reminding you of the gospel of grace and initiating a response in you toward Jesus? Don't miss God, his truth, and his kingdom while counting how many times the name of Jesus is mentioned in a Christian song. Know the issue and learn to discern. If all it takes to convince you that a song is "Christian" is knowing that it mentions Jesus, the CCM audience and the industry that feeds it are at an all-time low.

Anyone can put the name of Jesus in a song. Only a serious follower can possess a comprehensive kingdom perspective. Only a living being following in the new way can think, imagine, and create music and lyric in a way that faithfully represents Jesus and his kingdom. And only a Christian can listen to such music and discern its truthfulness and faithfulness. With ears to hear, listen.

In closing, I like what I'm hearing the latest movement of bands and artists say: "Christianity is my faith, not my musical genre."

As this book is being revised and updated, so-called worship music is enjoying a revival of sorts within the church in America, especially among those who purchase contemporary Christian music. The irony is almost not worth noting, yet it is difficult to resist. The popularity of worship among those whose lives are to be defined by worship deserves some reflection.

There are a few important points to note before we begin. First, to speak of worship revival and popularity is to recognize a renewed enthusiasm for *musical* praise and worship. Second, this revival/popularity is getting lots of help from marketing forces within the Christian music industry. Worship music now accounts for 30 percent of the market. Anytime numbers this dramatic appear, the question of the chicken or the egg gets revived. Which came first, authentic worship that industry has followed or authentic industry that worship has followed? I don't have the answer. Neither am I sure it's necessary to attempt to find one. It does, however, make me want to freshly examine what stewardship of the musical praise response ought to look and sound like.

WHAT IS WORSHIP?

It seems to me that true worship happens when a humbled heart draws near to God and sees reality as God sees it, as much as is humanly possible. In the center of this kind of worship, few human illusions exist. They can't breathe in that environment. There's too much Spirit and Truth to accommodate them. The rule and reign of God shout and whisper, circling a person with majesty on one hand and minutiae of detail on the other. The relentless, patient tenderness of this knowable God is overwhelming. He is a God who creates and relates, who talks to his creation, walks with them, and rescues them from sin and death and indescribable wrath. The worshiper knows that everything, everywhere, good and true, is of grace. It's all a gift. And because it is, the worshiper responds by thinking, feeling, speaking and acting on the truth that all honor, thanks, praise, and glory belong to God and God alone. The object of worship is always specific: the tri-personal God—Father, Son, and Holy Spirit.

Praise and worship *as a response to grace* is the starting place for thinking about worship in any form, including music. Where the discussion of worship begins and ends with music, there will always be foolishness, error, and strife.

Worship is the way followers of Jesus say yes to the truth of God's existence, his authority, his loving creativity, and his excellence (or glory). Consider the apostle Paul's own words from Acts 20:24: "However, I consider my life worth nothing to me, if only I may finish the race and complete the task the Lord Jesus has given me—the task of testifying to the gospel of God's grace." This is the path of all authentic followers of Jesus. God's grace is a certainty. It comes to people via storytelling and storied living through the life of the Teacher and Master, Jesus. He amazes people and thaws them out to feel wonder again. And so they praise God. This is the why of worship.

How can a student-follower not worship? For Christians, it is a fact that

God is Creator and re-Creator. We tell him, "You alone are worthy of worship. Your excellence compels us to speak and sing this certainty back to you, to say yes with our hearts, lips, and hands what is already a yes existentially." Christians believe that you can't watch God work and not be moved to ...

... in spite of my own wandering affections, I return to the truth that, for a follower of Jesus like me, worship does have a fixed starting place. It begins as an expression of belief in a very particular and certain trust: God is and always will be. This reality defines and frames life. Because God is, I cannot live as if he is not. I must live in response to his existence and his revelation of himself. My response is either cooperation or rebellion. It seems there is no neutral ground at the feet of God. I remember what God said about himself in the Old Testament book of Exodus: "I am the LORD your God, who brought you out of Egypt, out of the land of slavery. You shall have no other gods before me" (Exodus 20:2-3).

It seems that if I aspire to authentic worship, I'll have to begin by taking God at his word. My worship of God will only be good if I've heard God speak in Spirit and in truth and then use his thoughts as my starting place. Something like: "Yes, you are the Lord my God, Creator and Redeemer. You are the One who gave me freedom, who saved me from sin and death. You are the One who acted in history through Jesus to call a tribe of people to yourself. I will have no other gods before you. My heart is an idol-maker—a god-maker. Forgive me and help me. Create in me a clean heart and renew my ways. I acknowledge that you alone define reality. Help me know this reality, live within it, and promote its good agenda."

Worship as a Response

As I mentioned a moment ago, musical worship is a successfully marketed product. To draw attention to this does not mean I think all successfully marketed worship product is inauthentic. I haven't the desire or the ability to make such a judgment. What I can do, though, is contrast worship as a response with worship as a marketable commodity. The road to a good assessment and conclusion begins with the work of defining the various ways musical praise response is created.

The first is *spontaneous*. By this I mean a praise response that is unplanned and unrehearsed. For example, I love eating Vietnamese spring rolls with lots of hot-pepper sauce. Often, after the first few bites, I'm so overcome with gratitude that I shoot a hand up and praise God in the restaurant. I am completely sincere in this and usually not conscious of the "Thank you, Lord!" that bursts from my mouth. In this same way, gratitude and music will partner: A child of God is overcome with gratitude and worships in spontaneous song in private or public. The point being, it isn't planned or scripted.

Whole groups of people erupt in spontaneous worship as well. Years ago, while I was performing at the Cornerstone music festival, a large circle formed within the audience. From the stage I could see their pleasure. Communion with God and one another was evident. After the concert ended, the circle of people remained. They danced and sang for several hours, improvising around the basic motif of our last song. They came to hear a band from California, but the Spirit sent them home "with gratitude in [their] hearts to God" (Colossians 3:16).

More recently I was at Laity Lodge outside Kerrville, Texas, participating in a retreat. We had just listened to some great teaching and stories. Earlier, Don Murdock, our director, had asked if I would close the session by playing an improvisational response at the piano. Usually, during the first few moments of improvisation, I feel very self-conscious. Every musical choice seems so calculated and glaringly loud and obvious. Not this time. I was bursting with response, and it poured out like fresh water. A note here, a chord there, each a sign, symbol, and celebration of the goodness and rightness of God. As the music lost shape and came to a close, I could feel the swelling wetness of eyes and the movement of ...

... ...gs with the power of God,
a tiny majesty
made good by the great from without.
Tower of strength
I bow at the curve of your feet.
And all things entrusted to me
[Oh, your mercy overwhelms me]
I lay before you.
You own them as you own me—
with all tenderness of possession—
a fullness of belonging.
What words do justice to the tears?
What words do justice to the love I feel?
It was you, O Lord, who brought
me out of the pit of slavery
where death framed my choices
into the glorious brightness
that is you and your ways of
making life.
Help me, O Lord, to receive life, and so,

make life from life,

to your honor, praise, and glory.

This is my prayer.

For me at that moment, worship was spontaneous. It could not be held back. Worship overtook my whole being.

Not all worship is spontaneous. Much of the church's musical worship is what I would call *directed* or *guided*. A musical leader directs worship by selecting the songs to be sung, by assembling and rehearsing musicians and vocalists, and finally, by leading the fellowship in singing. In directed worship, followers don't attend rehearsals to learn the music and lyrics; they learn them via repetition, both by repeating a lyric and melody within a song and through weekly experiences of the songs. As with spontaneous worship, it's good and natural for both musicians and nonmusicians to participate. No one is excluded.

Musicians steward the praise response in unique ways exclusive to their talents, gifts, and callings. They have the work of *composing* and *performing* music in response to grace and in service of their fellow followers of Jesus. Both of these tasks require skill, ability, training, and spiritual gifting. With respect to the arts, the biblical Story makes clear that it's God who gives these to his appointed people for his good pleasure and purpose in history. (For example, see Exodus 31:3; 36:1; and 1 Chronicles 25:7.)

In all these ways—*spontaneous, directed, composed,* and *performed*—the creation of praise and worship is a historical response to the grace of God. Earlier I wrote that true worship happens when a humbled heart draws near to God and sees reality as God sees it. This should be at the heart of all spontaneous, directed, composed, and performed musical worship. It should be foundational to leading God's people in musical worship. In the various ways we steward the praise response, each is about declaring loud and clear, "Jesus, you are my Lord and King. I walk with you in your ways. I proclaim your name and not my own. I recognize that your ways lead to life, not mine. I watch your word and work, and you are excellent in every way, worthy of all honor and praise. Thank you, Jesus, for inviting me to walk with you, for saving me from sin, death, and wrath. You are rightness. Thank you, thank you

A Huge Task That Requires a Huge View

In worship we testify to the good news of God's grace. This is a huge task. The link between grace and praise cannot be exaggerated. Praise is the pleasure of the whole tribe of Jesus followers and every living creature appointed to that task. It is never the sole work of one man or woman. It takes the whole distributed intelligence and passion of the body of Messiah to reach anything like faithfulness.

Faithfulness in the stewardship of the praise response requires a huge view of what is praiseworthy. Is your view of what is praiseworthy big enough? Does it range from the grace of salvation through Jesus, to the grace of human sexuality lived out in fidelity, to the grace of the brightness of the stars and planets above as markers of beauty and mystery? I ask out of love. A small view of the Word and work of God leads to a small view of what inspires worship. We worship God as Redeemer and Creator. This being so, each of us following Christ ought to see an ever-widening view of what is praiseworthy.

There is still more work to do in widening the view and opening the landscape of worship. In most followers' minds, praise has one location: the church sanctuary. They tie praise to place. I do as well, but the place I connect it to is the place of God, people, and place, which is everywhere and in everything.

The Word of God connects praise to all manner of place and circumstance. For example, praise is located along the road after encountering the Word and work of Jesus. Jesus told a paralyzed man, "Get up, take your mat and go home" (Luke 5:24). The man stood up and went home praising God (see verse 25). Daniel praised God in bed during the night after a mystery was revealed to him in a vision (see Daniel 2:19). In the book of Joshua, the people praised God after finding out there would be no war: "They were glad to hear the report and praised God. And they talked no more about going to war against them to devastate the country where the Reubenites and the Gadites lived" (Joshua 22:33).

And still more examples of praise: "On coming to the house, they saw the child with his mother Mary, and they bowed down and worshiped him. Then they opened their treasures and presented him with gifts of gold and of incense and of myrrh" (Matthew 2:11). "Then those who were in the boat worshiped him, saying, 'Truly you are the Son of God' " (Matthew 14:33).

Reading through these parts of the Story makes me wonder. *Where do I respond to the King?* As people mature as student-followers of Jesus, the location of worship should become increasingly irrelevant. The people of God are a living alleluia. We should think and act as such. One sad feature of commercialized and domesticated praise and worship is that there's often a loss of connection to real life. In real praise and worship, just the opposite is true. Followers worship because life in God's world testifies to an object of worship, the living God. His presence and provision keep stirring the need for response. This is why I champion expressions of praise born in community and encourage Christians to tell their own unique praise stories in song. Has God restored a son to a father? Sing about it. Has God rescued a woman from the destructive effects of drug addiction? Sing about it. Has God given a gathering of followers a place to meet in peace and beauty? Sing about it. God acts in history every moment of every day. Where are the songs?

A Marketable Commodity

Now we can turn to the idea and reality of praise and worship as a marketable commodity. This is where we acknowledge that musical worship can be

[text obscured]

g. For example, Christian record companies often record the praise responses of various Christian communities. They fund and create recordings that document what would otherwise happen without them anyway. Here, the companies function as archivists, not product development teams. What they archive is likely to be a combination of spontaneous and directed worship involving both musicians and nonmusicians.

Good also happens when musical composition is intentionally and authentically aimed at declaring the mighty works of God, his character, his faithfulness, and his ability to save. In other words, it tells the Story of God, people, and place. If people purpose to do this and work to share it with others in community, it's good work.

The dangers of distributing musical worship responses are real. The fact that people have personal musical preferences and that consumerism has worked its way into the airspace of God's people is key to understanding the dangers. My opinion is that whenever the discussion of worship is lowered to personal preference of musical styles alone, you know you've entered the belly of consumerism (even when there is an apparent theological or religious emphasis behind your preference). The reality is this: Worship music becomes suspect when we create acceptable, preapproved form and content that has little or no connection to music as a response to grace or music made in service of the saints with God as its object, such as addressing the true needs of a worshiping community.

Nevertheless, I repeat, we needn't waste our time judging who or what is authentic. Our time would be better spent encouraging followers of Jesus to create musical praise and worship for authentic reasons, in response to grace and for the service of the saints. This is primary. Dissemination or distribution of music should always be secondary to grace-inspired creativity declaring the excellence of God.

An unfortunate side effect of the commercial success of worship music is that it put the lyric debate on the back burner—or off the stove top altogether. For many Christian music consumers and industry people, the rise of worship music fulfilled the dream of easily identifiable Christian music. It is common for a community to have its own exclusive language and music, and as I pointed out in an earlier chapter, it can be an act of love to yield to this reality and write with language even the least mature can understand. Still, the stewardship of music on the whole is about so much more than this, and it is the "so much more" that drives this book.

In this chapter I've talked about the stewardship of the musical praise response as it relates to the music of the church. This is only one area of musical stewardship, albeit an important one. Followers of Jesus are called to be caretakers of creativity everywhere and in everything. The work of caring for music is vast and diverse, as are the places and reasons for worship. When well-meaning Christians champion present forms of worship music as being the pinnacle of faithfulness, I get worried that their enthusiasm encourages unfaithfulness in other important areas of musical stewardship.

Two points in closing: (1) A serious musical follower of Jesus ought to cultivate an expansive understanding of musical stewardship without ever abandoning the creation and care of music for the church, and (2) if enthusiastic musical worship in the sanctuary does not lead to enthusiastic and faithful following of Jesus in the everything and everywhere of day-to-day life, something has gone wrong. "True worship looks like love and demonstrates love to all those around us," says Jars of Clay frontman Dan Haseltine, who sings about that very goal in the band's single, "Show You Love." According to Haseltine, "The song was actually written as a response to the

From its beginnings over thirty years ago until the present moment, CCM has increasingly embraced the ways of the world in its business practices and looked to those outside the community of faith for inspiration and acceptance. From songwriting to production, from marketing and promotion to artist management, there is no corner of CCM untouched by the world's ways of thinking about the creation and business of music. Many of these ways reflect healthy stewardship principles that make good sense and are in sync with God's Word. Other practices and values are bankrupt, with no connection to biblical imperatives; they are, in the vernacular, worldly. Love for God and his kingdom requires that people accurately identify the anti-Jesus agenda, turn from it, and have nothing more to do with it.

However, accomplishing this with any degree of faithfulness will be next to impossible as long as the men and women of Christian music see worldliness only as acting wrongly, rather than *imagining* and *thinking* wrongly.

The biblical Story speaks of worldliness as imagining and thinking wrongly. It teaches that the fruit of wrongly using the mind and its ability to dream is acting wrongly. As long as Christians view worldliness first as acting wrongly, which is tied to a short list of infractions such as adultery, drinking, smoking, and swearing, CCM's worldliness will go undetected. By focusing on a short list of destructive behaviors, we miss the most important idea of all: that worldliness is essentially sinful, futile thinking involving dependence on the world rather than on God. Worldliness, to draw a familiar biblical parallel, is about trusting in Egypt's horses, horsemen, and chariots instead of the Holy One of Israel. It's about trusting in the world or some other source for your provision and your meaning.

Scripture defines *world* in three ways: (1) the earth as a place created by God the Creator, (2) all the people groups of creation, and (3) all the ways of thinking and doing that are contrary to God's ways of thinking and doing. The first two definitions refer to our Father's world, a world that is ours to enjoy, care for, and transform. The last refers to the world of sin and Satan (the Twisted One), a world of thought and deed that the Bible instructs us to avoid at all costs. As we examine this world, we will discover whether there's any degree of truth in Steve Camp's charge that CCM "has gone too far down the wide road of worldliness."[1]

THE VALUES AND MEANING SYSTEMS OF THE WORLD

If you don't spend a lot of time in academia or reading books of a theological or sociological nature, the word *modernity* may not be part of your day-to-day vocabulary. It is, however, a word that all Christians in our time should know and understand. Its history and meaning have powerful consequences for everyone in Christian music. *Modernity* is a word that describes many of the values and meaning systems of the world that shape modern life, especially those still controlled and directed by baby boomers and the generation before them. Another pulse to life is loosely described by the term *postmodern*. However, I will not go down that rabbit trail at this time. Perhaps in another book.

The ideas and value systems of modernity dramatically affect everyone, including Christians—perhaps Christians most of all. According to author

John Seel, "Long before modernity changes the doctrinal content of belief, it alters one's assumptions about how life is to be organized day to day."[2] Once our assumptions about life are altered by what is valuable and meaningful to the world, and society is transformed by all ... . persons belief and trust in God.

A look at Reality Check, a young band I interviewed in April 1998 that disbanded later that year, will illustrate how modernity can sneak up on sincere people attempting to do good things in the name of Jesus.

Reality Check

Prior to signing a major record contract with StarSong in 1996, Reality Check had established itself as what many considered a potent and viable youth-oriented music ministry. On their own, with very little help from the CCM system, they were able to acquire a tour bus, a sound system, and stage lighting, and then eventually develop a sizable audience for their music—something most groups are incapable of doing without the help of a major label. Most important, on their own, apart from the CCM system, they were able to spend a good deal of quality time with their audience developing community and significant, lasting relationships.

In Reality Check's 1998 press kit, the band voiced clear and definitive ideas about the importance of their relationship with the audience and what it meant to minister to them:

> We don't want to come in and do an intense show, get everyone pumped up and then leave them hanging. We want to see kids saved,

but then we want to make sure they have Bibles and other materials, and that they get plugged in somewhere where they can grow. We like the Billy Graham model of ministry where people get saved, get counseled, have follow-up, and get planted in local churches.

In April 1998 I asked the band if signing with a major label, a manager, and a booking agent had altered their ministry at all. What you will hear in their responses reflects the influence and fruit of modernity. Listen closely.

Chris Blaney: "Before we were signed, we were able to spend an hour or two after a concert playing basketball with all the guys. It used to be we would sit and hang out, meet friends, and be able to spend what I would consider more quality time with people we've just met at the concert."[3]

Rod Shuler: "It's harder now to connect with the people. In the past we would have a day or two to hang out and really build some relationships, but now it's like we do a show and we're on the bus and headed to the next city. That's been very hard for me personally."

I asked Rod why the change in ministry philosophy. "It's happening," Rod said, "because we're doing so many dates now because we're trying to broaden our ministry. The thing is, you don't want to have to sacrifice, but you almost have to in order to meet a wider audience."

According to band member Nathan Barlowe, "The advantage of being with a label is that they are going to get you to more people so your ministry is able to grow."

The Definition of Success

Before we analyze what we've heard, let me ask some questions: What is most valuable and meaningful to the world: the concept of more or the concept of less? More, of course. How is growth defined? Is it the quantity of growth or the quality? With few exceptions, it's quantity. The more of any product consumers buy—whether it's a ticket to a concert or a new deodorant—the more successful the product is considered to be by the world's standards.

Before the days of mass communication and worldwide travel, our definition of *more* was generally kept in check by practical limitations. People

[text obscured] move on quickly to maximize their influence. The fact that we as people are largely unrestricted in our travel takes over our thinking and redefines the way we choose to live out our callings. When people finally stop to think and talk to God about important matters, they find that the values and meaning systems of modern life have chiseled away at their own core values and beliefs. They usually find out the hard way that having the ability to do something doesn't necessarily mean they should do it.

Have you ever wondered why people living in a society filled to the brim with time-saving devices and systems have absolutely no time for one another? The reason is fairly simple. To a man with a fax machine or an e-mail account, everything looks like important and urgent correspondence. But it's not. The same holds true for the good but biased support structure surrounding today's performing artists. To a booking agent everything looks like a potential concert date. To a manager everything looks like a strategy or a career opportunity. And to a publicist everything looks like an opportunity to publicize or maximize an artist's appearances. Yet in the economy of God, everything is not a potential concert date, a career opportunity, or an opportunity for publicity.

No Christian enterprise, including an eight-member, modern rock band with an evangelism emphasis, is beyond the power and corruption of modernity's touch. Good people who love God start out with a kingdom perspective that recognizes the value of spending "quality time with people," and they end up finding it hard to "connect with the people." This happens because modernity has reshaped their kingdom thinking into its own image under the guise of broadening their ministries. Os Guinness stated it well. "Under the influence of modernity, we modern Christians are literally capable of winning the world while losing our own souls."[4]

To borrow from author/teacher Dick Keyes, "The goal in life isn't to just accomplish many things." Nor is it just to accomplish many things for the Lord. "Life," says Keyes, "is first to be a certain kind of person before God."[5] The kingdom perspective of growth certainly allows for and encourages quantity, but it does so without ever defining growth strictly in terms of quantity. God's Word emphasizes quality growth. The size of the tree is far less important than the fruit the tree bears. This is why the "more" of ministry is always connected to a greater *quality* of fruit and not just a greater quantity of people. Broadening one's ministry will always be about faithfully loving and serving those within arm's reach long before it's about casting bigger nets.

What all artists (not just Reality Check) find out sooner or later is that signing with a major label and taking on a booking agent, a manager, and a publicist are not neutral choices. Each of these businesses or services is a legitimate calling, but we must never forget that they each have ideologies deeply influenced and shaped by modernity. When overseen by a comprehensive kingdom perspective, these services can be used for tremendous good—and often are. Yet by forgetting modernity's power and ignoring the core ideologies present within created things, we risk becoming something entirely different from what we faithfully set out to be. Even more frustrating is that we often become something we don't want to be and do things we don't want to do— and unfortunately, some do all of this in the name of ministry. If you search the biblical Story for examples of more ministry as defined by quantity alone, you will be hard pressed to find any. But if you look for scriptures encouraging people to a greater quality of serving (ministry), you will be busy for days.

While Jesus lived and walked among us, he could have had it all and done it all. He could have been king. He could have healed everyone and fixed every problem, but he didn't. He was on a specific mission, and he stayed his course. Jesus knows firsthand that the pace and pressures of modern life

...none of it. The kingdom he came to establish was and is a kingdom upside down from the values and meaning systems of the world. It has a completely different set of facts, values, cares, and commitments.

"Modern life," says Os Guinness, "assaults us with an infinite range of things we could do, we would love to do, or some people tell us we should do. But we are not God and we are neither infinite nor eternal. We are quite simply finite."

"Yet," offers Guinness, "as we make our contribution along the line of our gifts and callings, and others do the same, there is both a fruitfulness and a rest in the outcome. Our gifts are used for the purpose for which they were given us. *And we can rest in doing what we can without ever pretending we are more than the little people we plainly are*" (emphasis added).[7]

We can do no better than to turn again to Jesus on this topic, recognizing that the Lord who gave the commandment to his disciples to "go" (Matthew 28:19) is the same Lord who told his disciples to "stay" (Matthew 26:38). In God's kingdom there is time enough for everything. In the world, under its ways of thinking and doing, there is never time enough.

Who's in Charge Here?

"The citizens of Our Time," charges David Wells, "actually believe so little in God because they believe so much in what is modern."[8] It may be difficult at first glance to see how a statement like this could even apply to the artists, industry, and audience of CCM. After all, the community openly professes that it believes in God a great deal, not a little, and that its main purpose in using what is modern (such as technology and corporations) is to disseminate an important combination of music and message. Would they ever say they actually *believe* in what is modern? Modern techniques, methods, systems, and technologies are only tools to them—or are they?

It's long been obvious that contemporary Christian music believes in the powerful tool of celebrity, but this was never more obvious than at the 1998 Gospel Music Association Dove Awards telecast. Six months prior to the April 23 broadcast, Frank Breeden, president of the Gospel Music Association at the time, announced the GMA's intention to "follow the example of other highly rated awards shows and get a great host."

"Viewers will see our artists at their best," Breeden explained, "but when it comes to presenters, and hopefully sponsors, they will be looking at known quantities."[9] Those "known quantities" turned out to be John Tesh and Naomi Judd. To sweeten the pot, Whitney Houston was added to the bill as the evening's star performer. Tesh's profession of faith in Christ and his experience as a co-host of *Entertainment Tonight* made him an obvious celebrity choice, not to mention that he had recently begun to promote his own music in the CCM arena. While Tesh showed himself to be a more than capable host, Judd's actions and comments caused some GMA members concern. In addition to little things such as mispronouncing the name of the 1997 New Artist of the Year, Jaci Velasquez, Judd's theology of gospel music worked its way into the event and the media coverage as well. According to Judd, "We've got to get people to realize gospel music is not about this uptight religiosity stuff. It's fun and it's cool. Jars of Clay opened for Sting last year."[10]

Without wanting to come off as uptight and religious, I can't help but ask, Is the Christian music industry's motivation for creating and promoting "gospel" music to show the world that gospel music is "fun" and "cool"? I know it can be fun, and I suppose it could be cool, but is this why Christian music people do what they do? Does this articulate their calling? Did Naomi Judd, as host of the GMA Dove Awards, faithfully represent the truest and best motives and intentions of the community? And if String's "…"…

…, Judds, and Houstons celebrity yield? According to Schmitt, "The show only drew about half the audience it got last year [1997]. The Dove Awards got a 0.5 rating this year; last year: a 0.9 rating."[11] In other words, following "the example of other highly-rated awards shows" did not produce the results the GMA wanted, which was and is to increase the exposure of gospel music. They're trying to broaden the ministry to include more people, which is not a bad thing in and of itself. How, why, and when they (or any of us) do it is another matter altogether.

What concerns me greatly is how quickly we (myself included) can bet on the power of a person's celebrity without giving more than a passing prayer and acknowledgment to the power of God. And not just the power he demonstrated in creating our world or in feeding the five thousand, but in the passion and wisdom of the Cross.

THE WISDOM OF THE CROSS

The wisdom of the Cross is foolishness to the world. Sadly, its grand significance is often lost on Christians as well. Without the wisdom of the Cross, we will lack the spiritual vision to see what we need to see. We will see celebrity as the answer, and we will see more quantity as somehow more profitable than less quantity but greater quality. The wisdom of the Cross is paradoxical and upside-down from the wisdom of the world. For example, the first shall be last and the last shall be first…whoever wants to save his life must lose it…while we were enemies of God he saved us…God rejects the prideful success but receives the humbled failure.

On the cross Christ looked like a loser, not the Almighty—and certainly not a king. He looked like a crazy fool, not the Son of God. He looked like a man who needed a celebrity to get him off the hook. He was vulnerable to the point of death. But things were not as they seemed. There was a secret wisdom to Christ's cross. Out of the apparent defeat of the cross came an amazing victory. Three days later he was alive, sin and death were forever defeated, and the gospel of grace and the kingdom at hand became a tangible reality. Who knew? God knew, that's who! God still knows in our time, and he is still at work in an upside-down manner.

The wisdom of the Cross is the wisdom to see its connection to reality, to real life. On the cross it looked as if the Father had abandoned Christ. Three days later Jesus was vindicated. What if the greatest thing the Dove Awards could do for the kingdom of God was to appear to fail by the world's standards of success? Would we be willing? I would like to propose that those in charge do just that. Give it up. Rethink the whole affair. Perhaps if the CCM community were to face this kind of Good Friday reality [the appearance of failure], they would then taste of "Easter-morning possibilities that few have dared to hope for [true success]."[12]

In his book *The Mystery of the Cross,* Alister McGrath writes,

As Good Friday gave way to Easter Day, the experience of the absence of God began to assume new significance. Where was God? And as those bystanders watching Christ gazed proud, looking up to the heavens for deliverance, they saw no sign of God and assumed he was absent.… The presence of God was missed, was overlooked, was ignored, because God chose to be present where none expected him—

in the suffering, shame, humility, powerlessness and folly of the cross of Jesus Christ.[13]

What if the GMA/CCM community were to ~~~~ ~~~~~~ ~~~~ ~~~~ ~~~~~~ a moment to outline a new and better way to communicate what their community is doing with the call to music? Rather than trying to show the world they can be cool, what if they were to show they can be fools for things worth being foolish for? Perhaps God would be present in their shame, humility, powerlessness, and folly. Perhaps in this way they would broaden their ministry, their service to the church and the watching world.

As Mark Shaw has wisely pointed out, "God's way of working in the lives of those he loves as his children…is to bring them low in order to raise them high. The pattern of Christ's life, spelled out in the Gospels and summarized in Philippians 2:1-11, is the pattern of humiliation and exaltation. This is God's pattern for us as well."[14] The reality of this pattern is why Christian theology must be undergirded and deeply informed by a theology of the Cross.

The people of contemporary Christian music should neither lose hope nor allow themselves to be deceived. Remember:

> The crucified and risen Christ is at work in the weakness of the church,
> preparing to show his strength. Likewise, the crucified and risen Christ
> passes judgment upon the church where she has become proud and
> triumphant, or secure and smug, and recalls her to the foot of the cross,
> there to remind her of the mysterious and hidden way in which God is
> at work in the world.[15]

In order to possess the vision necessary to see where God is at work, many in the CCM community will have to rethink their ideas about what constitutes God's blessing—or God's movement.

Perhaps a blessing is anything that frees us from the grip of pride and self-sufficiency and drives us into the embrace of Jesus. God's work and movement can look as much like failure as it does immediate success. This being so, professing Christians must be careful not to err by saying that anything that looks like failure must not have God in it, and anything that looks like success surely has God in it. This is a false view of life in the kingdom at hand.

Seeking the Truth

I have yielded to Steve Camp's language of "worldliness" to respectfully examine his challenge. *Worldliness* is a term the church is accustomed to. For those readers unfamiliar with such inside language, let me redirect. What worldliness aims to describe more than anything is rebellion and contrariness to the way to be human that Jesus modeled. In this way, worldliness is always contrary to the Jesus agenda in the world. A study of what Christians call the Gospels will introduce you to what I'm getting at here. (See the words of Jesus in the New Testament books of Matthew, Mark, Luke, and John.)

Any serious search for worldliness—or an anti-Jesus agenda—within CCM must consider the possibility that the ideas and systems of the world may have succeeded in transforming the community more than it has transformed the world. Even more serious is the possibility that what Titus 1:16 says about non-Christians applies to many people in CCM as well: "They claim to know God, but by their actions they deny him." Love for God requires that people seek the truth in these matters.

Worldliness exhibits self-centeredness. Unlike godliness, which acknowledges that only God can be at the center of his creation, worldliness places humans at the center of the universe. Whereas godliness recognizes that all human thoughts are to be judged against the thoughts of God and the new way Jesus modeled, worldliness encourages the judgment of human thoughts against fallible human standards. Worldliness is the "way that seems right to a man, but in the end it leads to death" (Proverbs 14:12). W

...cuts, and he does the same with people today. Imagine how different history would be if Jesus had traded the hard way (the Cross) for the easy way (an earthly crown). This is the temptation people face daily. Recognize this reality and be prepared for it. People who profess to follow Jesus must live by the management principles of Jesus, not those of Satan the liar. The management principles of Satan are the same ones Jesus declined in the desert. They are, as Dorothy Sayers wrote in the play *The Man Born to Be King*, "fear and greed and the promise of security."[17] Just as Jesus rejected these, so should all people.

In his book *The Jesus I Never Knew*, Philip Yancey writes:

To its shame, Christian history reveals unrelieved attempts to improve on the way of Christ. Sometimes the church joins hands with a government that offers a shortcut path to power. "The worship of success is generally *the* form of idol worship which the devil cultivates most assiduously," wrote Helmut Thielicke about the German church's early infatuation with Adolf Hitler. "We could observe in the first years after 1933 the almost suggestive compulsion that emanates from great successes and how, under the influence of these successes, men, even Christians, stopped asking in whose name and at what price."[18]

This is not to take a cheap shot at CCM by making comparisons to Hitler. It is simply a reminder that people can never afford to stop asking, "In whose name and at what price?" To succumb to worldliness is to make this error. That's why the people of CCM should take Steve Camp's charge of worldliness very seriously.

Aware of the Danger

The systems, philosophies, and methods of the world are not inherently bad, and involving oneself with them does not necessarily have to lead to worldly imagining, thinking, and behavior. It's only when we allow these ideas to reign freely, unchecked by biblical, Jesus ways of being and doing that they contribute to our worldliness. When Christians interact with the world's systems and ideas, there will be times when their ideological biases will be at odds with biblical views. When they are, we should identify them as such. When we fail to do so, we irresponsibly acquiesce to ideas and positions incongruent with who and what we are as Christians. To do this is to succumb to an agenda other than the one we profess to live by. This is how the world contributes to a person's darkness. It is sinful to allow these incongruent ideas to set the agenda for life, for music. I would argue that CCM has in fact allowed this to happen.

Remember, every idea and system we use in Christian music comes with creational integrity and an ideological bias. Artistry has a bias, the corporation has one, marketing has one, radio has one. Everything has one, and they're all predisposed "to construct the world as one thing rather than another, to value one thing over another, to amplify one sense or skill or attitude more loudly than another."[19]

Is it possible that people in positions of leadership in CCM have been too comfortable with the world's ways of thinking, being, and doing? Have they mistakenly handled the world's ways as if such ways were neutral and void of ideology—as if these ways and tools possessed no creational integrity of their own, no ideological bias? Have they viewed the world's systems, techniques, and methods as simple, neutral tools with which to spread the good news of the kingdom? Have workers and artists in the Christian community missed the idea that even the simplest of tools—a hammer, for example

an ideal

any deviation in agenda from the Jesus agenda for the human family is too much.

After a speaking engagement, I typically enjoy a time of talking with members of the audience. Without fail, there are Christians in the audience who know my history with Christian music, and they ask one question in particular: "Charlie, are there people who are into contemporary Christian music for the ministry, or is everybody in it for the money?"

Yes, there are people who are into Christian music for the ministry, and, no, not everybody is in it for the money. But it's also truthful to say that, yes, everybody's into CCM for the ministry, and, yes, everybody is in it for the money.

It all depends on what you mean by "in it for the money." This phrase can mean that you have no other reason for doing Christian music than to get rich, or it can mean that you are a steward over good products that you sell to your community in exchange for money that you then reinvest in the community.

There's also more than one way to interpret "into CCM for the ministry." It doesn't necessarily mean you do it without expecting to get paid. Does ministry or service place anyone beyond the constraints and conventions of the culture in which they are attempting to serve? No, it doesn't. People are called to a life of serving others wherever God's people are—and that includes Fortune

500 companies, the grocery store, or a coliseum full of ticket-buying music lovers.

The issue is not a struggle between money and ministry. It's whether we will choose to serve ourselves or serve God and others wherever God puts us, with however much money he puts in our pocket. The question is not, "Charlie, are there people who are into contemporary Christian music for the ministry, or is everybody in it for the money?" The question is, To what or to whom have any of us given our trust, our allegiance, our affections, and our worship?

Many CCM critics and loyal listeners have oversimplified the issue of money and business to an unrealistic degree, creating in their minds an unholy alliance between ministry and money. Friends, there is no unholy alliance here; just foolish sinners. When money and business challenge us to refuse the good we know we ought to do, and we fail to do God's will, it's because we are sinful, selfish people who let another dark agenda get the best of us.

PROFIT AND THE HEALTH OF THE ECONOMY

The biblical Story has much to say about profit and wealth. Even Jesus emphasized productivity. The more uncommitted resources present in a community, the healthier the economy of that community. Extra uncommitted resources allow for the funding of important new ideas and dreams that are beneficial to society, important in telling good stories in the world. These ideas often reflect core values outside of any consideration of profit and wealth. For example: caring for those who cannot care for themselves, funding churches and crisis pregnancy centers, and offering academic scholarships. Profit ensures the presence of extra uncommitted resources, which in turn ensures that money is available for worthwhile endeavors that don't pay their own way. The bottom line is that capitalism (in theory) encourages profit, and profit, when used well, can create and support many good things, including the ongoing telling and living out of the Jesus Story and his agenda for life.

By definition, *capitalism* is an economic system fueled by supply and demand. When fans rush to the stores to buy a new CD

In her book *No Compromise,* Keith's widow Melody Green explained that "Keith figured most people knew the going price of recordings in the bookstores and understood that making records was very expensive. What he actually set up was an honor system of payment—trusting that if someone could afford to buy one they would."[1]

In spite of his good intentions, Keith found himself wrestling with the apparent contradiction inherent in this approach: "My whole reason for giving the album away is that I love people! Of course I don't want to see 50,000 people send in nothing. At the same time I don't want people to feel that I'm doing this to get a donation, or that they have to send in a donation."[2]

Keith didn't want anyone to feel that he was giving the album away in order to get a donation. Yet he willingly admitted that he wanted them to send in something. The knot of contradiction Keith tied himself up in is very common for people who wrestle with issues of ministry and commerce. A ministry that begins with the admirable intention of living out a genuine love for people and an utter dependence on God quickly becomes caught up in the contradiction that *no one has to send money/someone has to send money.* Getting trapped in this impasse is completely unnecessary. God in his wisdom has given people sufficient guidance to understand the relationship between labor and what it provides—it is his gift to the human family. Solomon spoke to this in Ecclesiastes 5:18-19:

> It is good and proper for a man to eat and drink, and to find satisfaction in his toilsome labor under the sun during the few days of life God has given him—for this is his lot. Moreover, when God gives any man wealth and possessions, and enables him to enjoy them, to accept his lot and be happy in his work—this is a gift of God.

Because many followers of Jesus fear that money and success will become their bottom line, they often try to arrange their lives to keep these things from ever tempting them to sin, to choose contrary to the way of Jesus. This pseudo-spiritual reaction to money and business will never produce lasting fruit. God has most definitely called followers of Jesus to live in the world with all its challenges and complexities.

Instead of living in response to the grace of God, people often make fear-based assumptions that leave them tangled up in semantic knots similar to the one Keith Green experienced. This kind of thinking also leads to very unproductive compartmentalization. If people fail to bring the whole of Scripture and the history of the saints to bear upon their thinking about money and ministry, they will never find sufficient truth to free themselves.

"Those that don't have anything can get an album for nothing," Keith Green declared from the concert stage. "And those that have little can get it for little. We believe the gospel's been getting a little too commercial. So, we wanted to uncommercialize our part of it."[3]

Keith's words reveal a common error we can all learn from. By stating that "we wanted to uncommercialize our part of it," Keith tried to remove himself and his ministry's monetary needs from the cultural sphere—a sphere God has clearly allowed for and uses for his kingdom purposes.

What is especially naive about this is the failure to see that the freedom to "uncommercialize" under the economic system of capitalism is only made possible by some number of people in society agreeing *to commercialize.*

Later, Keith adopted a different posture, starting with a letter of amends to Christian bookstore owners across America, saying, "I [illegible] information on how you can get it for whatever you can afford.'"[5]

This good choice is where Keith Green might have begun had he understood how even a seemingly principled choice could actually deprive his core supporters (the bookstores) of funding necessary to their own work. You can live within the culture in which you find yourself and still be as giving and altruistic as you care to be. Green eventually moved to such a position, which the above quote makes clear.

People in every generation will struggle with these issues. The struggle is good—as long as you really are seeking the truth and the will of God, as Keith Green sincerely was. It honors the Lord far more to struggle and agonize over these things, missing the mark here and there, than to float through life with your conscience, your emotions, and your mind on cruise control. There is absolutely nothing inherently wrong with Christian capitalism, even in the context of your ministry. In truth, we must participate in it, both out of necessity and in response to our calling to be God's people everywhere and in everything.

Where we go wrong in our association with capitalism is in our tendency to "evaluate life solely in terms of products and services, to assume that everything in life is amenable to capitalistic techniques, to grant efficiency the value of an ultimate criterion."[6] To err in this way, asserts author David Wells, is "to become so anthropocentric, so 'this-worldly' in spirit, as to be worldly in the biblical sense."[7] This is what we want to avoid.

Wells believes that "those who slide into worldliness this way are not likely to be conscious of the fact that they are doing so; the ways in which capitalism works are so much second nature to them that they will barely ever think about it. And since capitalism has been so extraordinarily successful, a person who prizes efficiency as an ultimate criterion will scarcely have any grounds on which to question its techniques."[8]

A look at the relationship between capitalism and technology will clarify Wells's point.

CAPITALISM AND TECHNOLOGY

Capitalism is one layer in the soil of modernity in which values contrary to God's ways often blossom. They are perennial, returning season after season. In addition, the soil of capitalism is made rich by technology. Technology exists to offer the "new" and to reinterpret the "existing." It exists to increase efficiency and productivity. Wherever technologies are championed and sold, the sales pitch is always deeply linked to the promise of a better life. Where technology achieves these goals, profits also increase. This is why capitalism has such an affinity for technology. Profits from present technologies produce capital to fund new technologies, and the cycle continues. And this is why technology has such an affinity for capitalism. They love to work together whenever possible.

As with capitalism, technology is not inherently bad, and Christians should not be afraid to take advantage of it for the benefit of all humankind—including telling the good Story of Jesus and the freedom and life he offers. Even so, like capitalism, technologies come with ideologies that cannot be ignored.

One of the greatest downsides to living in a capitalistic, technological society is not the creations themselves, such as the automatic teller machine, mass transit, cable television, or the Internet, but something far more insidious: technology's ability to shape our thinking in subtle, incremental ways over time, until our thoughts about something are different from what we previously thought. This is exactly what has happened with ill___l _____i__l

purchase a CD. Once bought, it could be copied and disseminated for free to millions via the Internet. For many people, music became free because the technology made it appear free.

The point for those interested in the Jesus way is that technology can shape a person's thinking in ways incongruent with God's agenda for humanity. If technology's efficiency and productivity help people achieve a desired end—such as a ministry goal they perceive to be good—people will naturally call that particular technology good. After all, it was the means to a good end. Once people perceive one efficient, productive technology to be good, they're inclined to give other technologies the opportunity to show that they, too, are efficient and productive. If and when the technologies prove themselves, it's likely people will call them good as well.

This is the precipice, the point of real danger. If followers of Jesus stop to think Christianly, they'll be safe. If they don't, they'll teeter or fall headlong into pragmatism. The problem has to do with the starting place. It's crucial to realize where good comes from. Is it God or technology? The point is this: Expediency, efficiency, and productivity are too weak to be the foundation for something as weighty as goodness or holiness. This is the real problem, and this is exactly how modernity (or so called worldliness) gets people so turned around in their thinking. Just because something works does not make it good.

Here's a rule of thumb: Expediency, efficiency, and productivity can be called good when and only when the good you think they've accomplished is tested against the biblical Story of what is good. This principle applies to everything in business and industry. All of business and industry must submit to the truth requirement—the rightness of God and his ways.

This is why capitalism is only good if it passes the test of Scripture, the test of thinking Christianly, the test of the Jesus agenda in the world. Most important, the tests of Scripture should be front-loaded, not back-loaded. People should be so biblically minded that they are always in the process of accepting or rejecting ideas and systems that come into their sphere of influence. People should never accept any of these ideas and systems outright without a front-end examination and understanding of their intrinsic ideologies— no matter how much potential for good they think these ideas have. This principle holds true for artists, radio, retail, television, print, record companies, new media, marketing, corporations, artist management, concert promotion, legal affairs, talent agencies—everything that has anything to do with Christian music as an industry or with Christians who create music everywhere and in everything.

The Corporation and the Record Company

A corporation is a legal entity capable of incurring liabilities, owning assets such as record and publishing companies, and engaging in specific activities such as producing, marketing, and distributing CDs. In the best-case scenario, a corporation exists to serve its community through products and/or services and to serve its shareholders by delivering a return on invested capital that exceeds viable alternative investments. A record company exists to produce, market, manufacture, and distribute the recorded performances of musical artists. Today, all the major Christian record companies are owned by entertainment corporations. Whereas the goal of a record company is to produce a quality, competitive, profitable music product, the goal of the corporately owned record company is this and more. Its goal is to produce a quality, competitive, profitable music product as well as a competitive return on the shareholders' investment.

A corporately owned record company is actually involved in the creation

......, ... g.o..... ....ase the competitive worth of the corporation.

Most record-company employees have a very special combination of passion and precision. Their passion for music and its place in the culture creates some amount of tension when it clashes with corporate culture. For example, at the heart of the record business is the idea of nurturing and developing musical artists so they will make long-term contributions to popular music. The pop history books are filled with examples of important artists, such as Bruce Springsteen and U2, who required time to develop before delivering on the potential people first saw in them.

But in today's world, corporately owned record companies have less and less time to develop and nurture talent. The focus has shifted from long-term potential to short-term profit. It's all about meeting and exceeding corporate projections. According to Don Weir of HFI Securities in St. Louis, "U.S. corporations have developed a myopic preoccupation with short-term results, with corporate policy shifts in many instances dictated by whether or not the next quarterly earnings report will be up and, if so, up as much as the shareholders and the general investing community expects."[9]

When your sales are tied to the stock market and the earnings estimates of prestigious market analysts, the pressure to produce results is intense. While it's essential for a corporation to serve its shareholders, Weir believes the drive to impress shareholders with ever increasing profit "has come dangerously close to supplanting not only the mission to serve their consumer-base, but their employees as well." Every savvy employee who's ever been "downsized" knows that the quickest way for a corporation to increase revenue is to eliminate overhead. When men and women are called upon to let good employees go in order to meet corporate and shareholder expectations, it is a difficult and unrewarding assignment.

While independent record companies may keep the passion for music alive, it's the corporately owned companies who define the record industry and ultimately acquire the most successful of the independents. Once acquired, the independent may incrementally morph into the image of the parent corporation until they are one and the same.

The Bottom Line

Christians must be cautious and vigilant when dealing with capitalism, the corporation, and the record company. It is sinful self-interest and the propensity of these three entities to shape life in ways out of sync with a kingdom perspective that causes Christian music so much trouble. Contemporary Christian music does not have to make money and success the bottom line in order to move within the business world and serve the musical and spiritual needs of the church and those curious about the Jesus way. The question does not have to be, "Are there people in CCM for the ministry, or is everyone just in it for the money?" Ministry (again, I'm talking service to others), compensation, and profit are not incompatible ideas. However, their compatibility depends on how ready and well-prepared people are to take on the challenge of living in a complex and crazy world concurrent with the presence of the kingdom of Jesus.

When CCM's sole purpose becomes economic success, without regard for God and his creation, the wants of a few will have eclipsed the needs of many. This is what the corporately owned Christian record company must guard against most of all. Christians are about—should be about—the needs of many, and this mission alone should define CCM in relation to money and the business of music.

It is important that the Christian music community and holders of investors to understand that the financial success of Christian music isn't what ensures human provision. It's not anyone's clever thinking, business deals, sacrificial "work for the Lord," position in the community, market share, or scratching of itchy ears that assures people they will be okay, that they will be taken care of, that they will have enough. God and God alone ensures this promise. To believe it requires faith and trust—taking God at his word. May God graciously give these to anyone who asks.

S ince beginning to work on the revised edition of this book, I've had the pleasure and privilege of traveling across the country promoting my book *New Way to Be Human,* doing concerts, and speaking to wildly diverse groups of people. Though I've traveled across the United States and back many times since moving to Nashville in 1989, this recent trip has revealed the biggest shift in public opinion regarding Christian music that I've ever seen. Several trends that began developing over the past several years have now resulted in full-fledged shifts in opinion, philosophy, and practice.

By leaving Nashville and traveling around the country, I see Nashville more clearly than ever. It's mainly only the people in Nashville, the hub of the world's Christian music activity, who are the real, enthusiastic champions of Christian music in its commercial forms. People outside Nashville are not as caught up in the frenzy. Don't get me wrong; many Christians still have their favorite Christian bands and artists. What's different, though, is that Christian music (as in contemporary Christian music as a genre) is no longer a default setting for the believer (listener or musician) who is interested in music. This, more than anything, may account for the diminished sales of Christian music over the last few years. As much as I want illegal downloading to stop, maybe, just maybe, other more sweeping cultural changes are contributing to a decline in support of CCM.

In fact, I observed that many followers of Jesus are moving from respect and appreciation for contemporary Christian music to disrespect and disinterest. It is meaning less and less to them. Much of today's audience is looking for meaning in community-based music—music and artists that do not smack of an entertainment corporation's heavy-handed marketing, imaging, and fear-based artistic tinkering. Because the music itself has meant less and less to its artists and corporate overseers, it naturally means less to the audience. Time and again, words and phrases like "authentic," "real," and "less manufactured" come up as people describe what they are looking for in music. Shawn Young, an instructor at Greenville College in Illinois who teaches the course "Philosophy and Ethics in Contemporary Christian Music," says that his students "see mainstream nonindependent Christian artists as timid with regard to taking creative chances.... They applaud those who operate on the fringes and hail them as relevant and 'authentic.' They value authenticity to the point of questioning the depth of those CCMers who would wear a mask and play a part just to sell the album."[1]

Finally, I think there has been a massive shift in the musicians themselves. Out of all the musical artists who are followers of Jesus that I've been meeting, and I'm talking the best and the brightest, only a handful have any interest in being a part of Christian music as an industry. These few want to love God and his church through music, which is excellent. The majority (easily 90 percent in my experience) want to take their art and worldview into the music mainstream via the independent ("indies") or major labels, which is also excellent. This particular impulse has always been present in contemporary Christian music. The difference today is that what began as a tiny seed is now a full-grown tree. The talent is leaving the CCM talent pool for an ocean of possibilities. This dramatic change in artistic priorities will alter Christian music forever. It already has. Just look at how the top artists on *Billboard*'s Christian charts also have mainstream chart-topping songs. So just how did this change in the artistic priorities and practices of today's young artists come about? To answer this question, let's take a few steps back.

Much of the impetus to write the original edition of *At the Crossroads* was born out of frustration. The Christian music community had done such a [illegible] fate was sealed. In what must be one of the world's greatest ironies, Christian music executives found themselves directed by non-Christian corporate executives to maintain simple "Christian" identity and to focus content and marketing on Christians. The mainstream corporations did not purchase these Christian record companies to have them duplicate the product development that a Virgin or Columbia Records was already engaged in. They purchased Christian companies to own that particular slice of the entertainment pie. Of course, entertainment corporations do occasionally tap the Christian market as a source of talent, as they do all genres. EMI's international push of Norah Jones from the jazz label Blue Note is no different in theory and practice than Stacie Orrico's crossover from the Christian label ForeFront to Virgin Records. In both cases, EMI corporate made a decision to uplift these acts and put "pop" money and influence behind them. The rub for followers of Jesus who believe they are to be direct representatives in the world is that they have to gain permission from the corporation to be what they're created to be. As a result, the corporation is given sovereignty, not God.

Since the original version of *At the Crossroads* was written, people who recognize the irony and vacant theology of this dynamic have grown increasingly intolerant of it. I understand. Having started my musical career in mainstream pop music, I empathize with young artists who want nothing more than to create art with a comprehensive view of musical stewardship, who want the freedom to be real people writing about everything in God's creation, who want to share their art with anyone and everyone. Several years ago I came to a point where I saw the culture of CCM (for the most part) as either unwilling or ill equipped to help those young artists. It angered and shamed me. How had people who profess to know the deepest secrets about how life is shaped come to such a place where they could not or would not help the best and brightest shine as true artists?

Things came to a head for me. I knew I couldn't continue to show up and collect my fees for producing records and return to my otherwise comfortable life. Certainly there was something I could do to contribute positive changes to the industry.

EXPERIMENTING ON THE CLOCK

I made my own (somewhat limited) attempt at being a part of the solution with an independent record company I started in 1995 called re:think. The mission of re:think was to take artists to the mainstream and Christian markets simultaneously. I created the re:think label to record and promote an extraordinarily talented and diverse, though like-minded, group of artists. I was looking for artists who, through their lives and music, demonstrated a unique equipping to speak to both the church and the watching world, without ever changing who God created them to be. They had to be interested in the same things Jesus said he is interested in and unapologetic in their commitment to creativity and the life of the imagination. In short, I was looking for artists who would say, " 'Christian' describes my faith, not my musical genre."

Like any other record company, re:think sought to form relationships with these types of artists with the purpose of recording and promoting them to the marketplace. What made re:think distinctive was its mission to *simultaneously* market and promote these artists to the Christian community and to the mainstream. My hope was that re:think artists would refresh the hearts and challenge the minds of Christians; replicate good, truth, and beauty; ask life-altering questions; tell the truth about humanity in our glory and our shame; and creatively enjoy what God had imagined and created through the gift of music.

Chordant (now known as EMI CMG) on the Christian side. Our mission was to be a record company, not a Christian record company that spent most of its money trying to reach the Christian consumer while dabbling in the mainstream. On the contrary, we were taking both sides very seriously, especially the mainstream, since the mainstream was where we had the most to learn. My small staff and I put together substantial marketing plans for both markets and set about the business of cutting a new trail, hoping to remain faithful to our mission. Unfortunately, we did get pegged as a Christian label and fought hard to overcome the marginalization that came with such labeling. I did not want to believe it at the time, but a good friend of mine, a manager of a well-known mainstream rock group, warned me, "If an act is distributed at all to the Christian market, then the act is Christian."

We worked with several key people at EMD and Chordant, whose knowledge and experience helped us navigate the massive organizational system that makes up pop music. Working closely with EMD's artist development reps, we arranged for price and positioning, co-op ad buys, radio-time buys, and listening posts—all with the purpose of encouraging mainstream retail stores to take Sarah Masen's music seriously. The reason some artists seem to have so much exposure in retail while others have little to none has everything to do with whether these marketing tools are budgeted for and maximized.

We hired independent radio promoters to work Sarah's record at adult alternative radio. In addition, we retained a national publicity firm to solicit mainstream reviews of her record. As a new label looking to add value to our product, we were the first record company in America to contact and partner with America Online to include an AOL installer on the CD-ROM portion of Sarah's CD. We set up and executed an extensive U.S. promotional tour for Sarah through Borders Books and Music. In some cities Sarah performed as many as four times a day, all for the purpose of exposing the mainstream community to her music. She played in retail stores, for mom and pop distributors, at EMD branch offices, at showcase clubs for retailers and radio influencers, for *Radio & Records* and for *Billboard*. She attended the Gavin Radio Convention in Boulder. In short, we attempted to do with Sarah what every pop label does with new artists. We promoted her to the music-buying public the best we knew how with the resources at our disposal. We believed in her and wanted her music and artistry to be taken seriously. The dream didn't last long. I could identify and develop great talent—great enough to create endless opportunities—but I could not compete with the entertainment corporations' money. Lack of capital did us in. We transferred ownership of re:think to EMI in 1998.

My friend, artist, producer, and filmmaker Steve Taylor, started his company Squint Entertainment in 1997 with a similar vision of contributing to music and culture. With financial backing from Word Records and mainstream distribution through the independent Alternative Distribution Alliance (ADA), Steve and his staff set to work marketing and promoting Sixpence None the Richer's self-titled album. They had a worldwide radio hit with the song "Kiss Me," bolstered by its inclusion on the soundtrack to the movie *She's All That.* Squint's staff worked diligently on the marketing and sales side to make sure Sixpence was taken seriously, while the band crisscrossed the nation and the globe promoting its music. Sixpence made many national television appearances on programs such as *The Late Show with David Letterman* and *Today,* and received a Grammy nomination for Best Pop Performance by a

Duo or Group with Vocal. In short, they were participating in and contributing to the culture at large. In 1999 Squint released a rock album by a group named Chevelle that was also marketed to mainstream audiences, finding video airplay on MTV. Today, Chevelle has a successful recording career with the CCM and mainstream music markets (in most cases simultaneously). That's not to say that albums or songs by Christian artists hadn't been promoted to mainstream audiences before or after these labels came in to being. It's just that the most prevalent model for mainstream promotion of Christian music has been one of a Christian label serving as the original label home of the artist and then partnering with a general-market label that handles the marketing and promotion duties—something generally known as "crossover." In the past the decision by labels to attempt crossover was usually made when an artist reached a certain sales figure—usually somewhere between five-hundred-thousand units and one-million units. This was the case with artists like dc Talk, Michael W. Smith, and the Newsboys. But getting to a certain sales threshold in the CCM marketplace is no longer the qualification for whether a mainstream label will partner with a Christian label. Tooth & Nail, a quasi-independent label (which is partially owned by EMI), for example, has attracted mainstream-label interest for a few of their artists without gold or platinum sales. Other smaller labels have done the same.

In today's environment of corporate ownership, the Christian record label is actually expected to be a talent scout for the whole corporation. If the Christian label hears a song or a particular artist that might translate well to a mainstream audience, the corporate owner wants to know about it, because the corporation's goal is exploitation of artist brands wherever it can be done, for the purpose of maximizing profit. With that said, aspiring artists still should not go to a Christian label if they really want to be on a mainstream label or make music for a mainstream audience. If an artist or group is on a Christian label, even one that is owned by a global music corporation, that artist or group will be marketed to a Christian audience. If at some point someone decides that an artist is making music that will compete in another market, then a label may pursue other opportunities for the artist. However, the primary purpose of the Christian record label, in the eyes of the corporate owner, is to capitalize on a niche market.

The Music-Makers

Because so many young, talented artists and businesspeople see the industry and genre of Christian music as irrelevant or unable to help them in their goals of making great music for any and every audience, many of them are bypassing the CCM system altogether and going directly to general-market labels, whether major or indie. Many others are simply working as independent artists, unaffiliated with a record label at all. Christian business people are creating indie labels that have no affiliation with Christian music, and they clearly want it that way.

Several years ago, Matt Odmark from Jars of Clay told me that taking our music into the world and not having to ask permission from the world to do it—moving beyond crossover—"may start with a group of people who firmly believe Christianity belongs right in the middle of rock'n'roll as much as Christianity belongs anywhere."[2] Matt's words have come true. This is exactly what has happened. But it's not a new story. It's only new to a thirty-five-year-old genre known as Christian or gospel music. People who profess to follow Jesus (or have some history with Judeo-Christian faith) have always been music-makers in the world. Not only have they been present in history but they've been significant history-makers—the very best in the world.

Let's begin with the historical Jewish character David, an artist-king, a

musician and singer of songs, a dreamer, a dancer, a man with an aptitude for
sheep. David held a high position in the economy of God, people, and place.
He was God's direct representative, working the planet Earth, the Milky Way,
tending the jazz of God. People still sing his songs

up the pop charts with songs that ask the best and most important questions
about what it means to be human. These are just a few of the music-makers
whose names are known around the world. Their fame does not make Jesus
relevant. He doesn't need their help. These artists are in fact relevant because
they have held together belief and musical creativity in a fashion that rings true
for many in the human family, Christian or not.

This is exactly what a new generation of followers wants to be about. In
this respect, what they desire is not new, but an old, old way in the world: to
be a faithful musical human on the planet and eschew all labels that diminish
what it means to be truly human and to truly love God and his creation. This
is the way things should be. This is the ocean too big for a glass, music too big
for a genre.

CARETAKERS OF GOD'S CREATIVITY

Part of a Christian's controlling story is that God has great patience—even for
people who create an alternate universe of *Christian* things to avoid being polluted by the world, turn and sell their companies *to the world*, and then fail to
contribute to the culture they profess that their God is Lord over. Given this,
you can imagine how a person involved in Christian music might be grateful
for a little patience from God.

Hopefully you've picked up on my agenda: to communicate that there are ways of being and doing that reflect God's ways better than others. Christians who create and care for music should move toward greater faithfulness, not less. This is one of the good goals of this book. Not only have I written for the church and the CCM industry, I have written for those who do not hold to the Jesus understanding of reality. Why? I don't want people to think they have understood the Jesus way when all they've really understood is the contemporary Christian music way. If I have not made the distinction between the two clear by now, I'm in trouble.

I've heard many critiques of Christian music over the years: It's not honest. It's copycat. It's propaganda, not art. It's escapism. It's just not good music...and so it goes. Unfortunately, many of the accusations are true, but especially true in the context of contemporary Christian music that was birthed as copycat music and not as true, honest, committed art making. (I say this with apologies to those who were authentic in the beginning.) This genre of music has never recovered from its beginnings. Given that, let's let it go and get back in the flow of history, along with the names I mentioned above, from King David to U2 and beyond. This is where the real music is and where the music is headed. Don't be completely rigid, though. These are transition times, which means that right now there are artists still recording for Christian labels who make vital and imaginative music. Be fair to them. If they really are good, say it. Don't punish them for where they are distributed. This guilty-by-association thing must pass. Judge them on their merit. For example, right now the critics are falling all over themselves anointing a young artist named Mindy Smith. She records for the infamous folk imprint Vanguard. I have to wonder if the critics would still be fawning over her if she had stayed at the Christian company, Word Music, where she began. Why don't we advocate more honesty from everyone—critics, artists, Christians, and those who don't share a belief in the Christian story? More honesty and charity on the side of everyone is just good for people and the planet.

Finally, accept no substitutes for good music or for the way of Jesus. This, too, is at the heart of why I've written this book. Don't fake it, and don't champion or enable those who do. Our time is a time of new opportunity. Every human has the opportunity to become God's direct

it is also unfortunate that people outside the tribe think that Jesus came to start a new religion. He did not. He also didn't come to create a two-hour-on-Sunday parasite culture that pious, religious types can paste on the side of their busy, status-quo lives. Jesus came to subvert every aspect of life and culture with the new way to be human and something he announced as *the kingdom*. As I've written elsewhere:

> The kingdom, or God's rule, is what brings a person's life into alignment with reality. To live in the kingdom way is to live a real and everlasting life, beginning the very moment you follow Jesus. This means that everything is overhauled or restructured to fit the kingdom way, the new way to be human. Knowledge, education, romance, marriage, sex, parenting, work, play, money, ambition, business, social services, caring for the earth, even being the church in the world—all of these areas and a thousand more now come under kingdom rule and authority. Following Jesus faithfully means seeing to it that all of these areas in our lives are subverted by the kingdom and rebuilt in the new way.[3]

Of course music and the business of it fits into this as well.

Whether you're reading this book as a follower or just a curious researcher, listen to Jesus's own words in the first four books of the New Testament. See for yourself what Jesus is interested in and question not only if it squares with commercial Christian music in general but if it squares with your own ways of being human. Anyone who has studied world history, or church history, knows that thirty-five years of misdirected musical stewardship is but a blip on the screen of the history of human failure. We will recover from this as better and more faithful people, eager to make great music as caretakers of God's creativity. Maybe you know how to help. If so, stand in the Story for a moment and see if life takes on a different look—one with the peace of reconciliation, meaning, and purpose. As you can tell from reading this book, people need all the help they can get in building a new community that takes the Story seriously and actually does what Jesus taught.

Each day in our lives will be a new adventure, dreaming for the good of people and place. There will be love and tears, kisses and hard work, good food and drink, children and laughter, quiet moments of knowing but not speaking. There will be the poetry of days as they whoosh by, and there will be music, new music made from the jazz of God and the dreams of living beings made in the image of God. And on the best days, it will be like a sweet, safe swim in the clearest of oceans.

Afterword to the Revised and Updated Edition

I am not exactly sure what it was about the experience that sent a wave of emotion over me. I know it had something to do with the way I have been wired to respond to beauty. It may be that I was experiencing the exhibition of a shared vocation executed with precision and excellence. But in the arena, I stood with my face raised to the rafters and let the tears roll down from the corners of my eyes, while thousands of voices raised in communal worship, sweet hallelujahs, and confident "glorias!" swirled around the concrete complex. It was a true fragment of Eden in what may have been an unlikely temple.

From that moment, the beginning chords of "Where the Streets Have No Name" moved people into a frenzy. I stood there and let the salt of my tears dry on my smiling face. "Glory be to God who gives us music, gives us voices to raise, and hearts to overflow." I let the sounds, the vision, and the movement swallow me like a giant fish. I was Jonah. Before that night I had looked back upon the vocation of Jars of Clay and sensed that perhaps we had wandered in the wrong places, but I was being given a vision, an affirmation, and a new appreciation for where God had taken us, and where he would have us go next.

⌒

In a small club in the heart of the Nashville entertainment district, a group of seasoned musicians/songwriters gathered for a night of soul music. I sat along the wall with the rest of my band mates and listened to the echoes of Motown—a foundational and highly influential stretch on the timeline of American music—come to life as if we had somehow stepped into a portal shifting through the '60s and '70s.

In a night of tributes, the greatest came when the musicians tipped their hats to Stevie Wonder in a heartfelt, gut-punch version of "Superstition." My eyes filled with tears. They were not the kind of tears provoked by a well-placed piano part during a sermon or an emotional string melody that breathes high above the choir on a Sunday morning. They were simply a response to a combination of inspired musical execution and performance connected to a brilliant musical creation. I was given a gift—something that worked as it should in a world defined by the things in it that are broken.

I shifted my gaze down the row to see what my fellow mates were getting out of the performance, and the row of wide and soggy eyes made it clear that we all were finding the joy of such an amazing musical liturgy.

It was as if God was tapping us on the shoulders and directing our focus toward something broken that he had just fixed. We were introduced to another character in the story of redemption, who reminds us that God is at work, doing things only he can do, acting in ways that have a pattern and resolution that he alone can see.

"Look at this," he was saying that night. "My kingdom is filled to overflowing with things like this, things that were worn and broken and are now restored." We worshiped: "To God be the glory; it is only by your hand that our understanding of time and its destructive ways would be harnessed and turned around to reveal that you, God, have made the presence of eternity restorative."

I am in a band full of people who resonate with God through things like movies, songs, and novels. Perhaps it is the way our hearts connect with the bird's-eye view of the way a relationship travels from the precipice of doubt and defense to humility and service, or simply the way a story unfolds to the clari

stripped away, allowing us to move one step closer to God, one step closer to a life of worship and a heart moved by hope. And hope is what faith feeds upon.

We spend far too much time lingering in a place of knowing that life is not as it should be, that the world is broken, and that our own skin, bone, flesh, and heartbeat are irregular and faint. We can lose hope; we can lose our compass and end up in places where worship of God takes a close second to an evening in front of late-night television. Many of the prophetic voices in music today, the voices committed to looking at their world and describing it, spend a great deal of time filtering their worldview through their understanding of this human reality. Hundreds of artistic expressions affirm this frailty. These expressions can fill every step of a journey, every beat, every chord and every melody, every stroke of a painting, and every string of dialogue in a great movie.

The world is frustrated, and given our experience in life, we should always expect the worst, the loneliest, the most destructive elements to win in the end. And so we brace ourselves for this impending outcome. And when the good guy wins in the story or when darkness is split and severed by light, we experience a sense of relief, a small reminder of what is true and what the gospel truly is about. Though we struggle to keep this truth in a place fit to lean upon, our day-to-day experiences usually cause us to forget, to lose hope and fall back into a self-protected life. We end up with a blindness to God's work and a focus on personal safety and comfort—a spiritual Prozac. Our lives are found passionless and sleepy. Our only hope of true awakening is when God, through his Spirit in his Word, reminds us that the gospel is true by way of small glimpses of things further along in the redemptive journey.

This awakening is the beginning of worship. It is here that we are able to shift our focus off ourselves and onto the hope of the kingdom that is already here and the kingdom that is yet to appear. And being connected to a group of artists who take seriously the role of elevating the gospel in the arts, and the arts in the gospel community, we want more than anything to have our hands in the telling of redemptive stories, in tales that might remind people that the gospel story is real and that we can be restored. Music, rather than being the act of worship, becomes the catalyst for worship. We remind people that there is a God worthy of our praise, worthy of our affection, and jealous for our love in the wildest and most wonderful of ways.

—DAN HASELTINE, Jars of Clay

Notes

Chapter 1: Voices at the Crossroads

1. Kathleen A. Ijames, Letters, *Calvin College Chimes* 92, no. 16 (January 1997): 5.

2. WAY-FM, "An Open Letter to the Christian Music Community," *CCM Magazine* 18, no. 11:128.

3. Scott MacLeod, *Snakes in the Lobby* (Nashville: Provision Press, 1997), 1.

4. MacLeod, *Snakes in the Lobby,* 3.

5. MacLeod, *Snakes in the Lobby,* 43.

6. MacLeod, *Snakes in the Lobby,* 43.

7. MacLeod, *Snakes in the Lobby,* 44.

8. Reverend Randy Campbell, Peoples Church, letter announcing termination of Jesus Northwest Christian music festival, November 1997, Salem, Oregon.

9. Steven John Camp, "A Call for Reformation in the Contemporary Christian Music Industry," letter written to CCM industry, October 31, 1997, www.worship.com/steve_camp_107_theses.htm.

10. Camp, "A Call for Reformation."

11. Camp, "A Call for Reformation."

12. Steve Camp, letter written to CCM industry, November 1, 2002, www.freshreleases.com/news/893.html.

13. Lindy Warren, "Album Lyrics Raise Questions: Lack of 'Christian' content complicates Dove Award eligibility, chart placement decisions," *CCM Update* 11, no. 35 (September 1997): 1.

14. Rick Anderson, quoted in Warren, "Album Lyrics Raise Questions," 5.

15. The term *gospel music* used throughout this chapter is meant to denote the whole of popular Christian music in America, from Southern gospel to CCM. While the Gospel Music Association (GMA) continues to perpetuate the term *gospel music* through its literature and events, the bulk of the Christian music industry is commonly known as CCM or contemporary Christian music.

16. Frank Breeden, quoted in Warren, "Album Lyrics Raise Questions," 5.

17. GMA Board of Directors and Dove Awards Committee, 1998 definition of gospel music, quoted in Lindy Warren, "GMA Defines 'Gospel Music': New criteria to determine eligibility for Dove Awards," *CCM Update* 12, no. 26 (July 1998): 1.

18. Mark Joseph, *The Rock & Roll Rebellion: Why People of Faith Abandoned Rock Music—and Why They're Coming Back* (Nashville: Broadman & Holman, 1999), 186.

19. Joseph, *The Rock & Roll Rebellion,* 216.

20. John Styll, quoted in Gospel Music Association press release, "Gospel Music Sales Are Rebounding; Several Artists Having Impact in Multiple Genres," January 7, 2004, www.gospelmusic.org/news/article.cfm?ArticleID=76.

21. Bill Hearn, quoted in Jeanne Anne Naujeck, "Christian Music Sales Lifted by Diversity," *The Tennessean,* sec. E, January 25, 2004.

22. Michael Janke, press release, "NewSong Wraps Up Winter Jam; Parts Ways with Reunion," March 17, 2004, www.cmcentral.com/news/1950.html.

Chapter 2: Getting the Story Straight

1. This chapter highlights three important ideas: (1) what Scripture calls the *kingdom of God*—On this topic I have borrowed liberally from my pastor Scotty Smith's enthusiastic teaching...

Subjects in His Kingdom," pt. 8, July 5, 1998.

3. Scotty Smith, unpublished sermon notes, June 21, 1998.

4. See Os Guinness, *The Call* (Nashville: Word, 1998), 31.

5. Guinness, *The Call,* 31.

6. From a mailer Ken Meyers sent out to his subscription list for the Mars Hill audiotape series. To receive a copy of "Life Work: On the Christian Idea of Calling," write to Mars Hill Audio, PO Box 1527, Charlottesville, VA 22902.

7. Elton Trueblood, *Your Other Vocation* (New York: Harper, 1952), 57.

8. Dan Haseltine, interview with the author, *Gospel Music Week,* April 20-22, 1998.

9. Charlie Lowell, interview with the author, *Gospel Music Week,* April 20-22, 1998.

10. Trevor McNevan, quoted in Jay Swartzendruber, "Thousand Foot Krutch: Tooth & Nail's Next Breakout Artist?" *CCM Magazine* 26, no. 6 (December 2003): 44.

Chapter 3: The Jesus Movement

1. Billy Graham, quoted in "The 'Jesus Movement': Impact on Youth, Church," *U.S. News & World Report,* March 20, 1972, 59.

2. Kenneth A. Myers, *All God's Children and Blue Suede Shoes: Christians & Popular Culture* (Westchester: Crossway, 1989), 155.

3. "The 'Jesus Movement,'" *U.S. News & World Report,* 60.

4. Historically, the influence on CCM's beginnings of the two theological positions mentioned here can be traced to the teaching of charismatic-affiliated pastors and leaders such as Southern Californians Chuck Smith of Calvary Chapel, Jack Hayford of Church on the Way, and John Wimber of The Vineyard, as well as Don Finto of Belmont Church in Nashville, Scott Ross of the Love Inn community in New York, and later, though no less significant, Louis and Mary Neely of The Warehouse in Sacramento, California.

A survey of thirty-five popular CCM artists and groups taken in April 1998 revealed that fellowship in a nondenominational setting was still very attractive to CCM artists. When asked, "What faith tradition best describes you?" 25 percent of those polled chose the term *nondenominational.* Another 25 percent chose the term *Baptist.* The next largest block, atypical of CCM's past, chose the term *Presbyterian* to describe their faith tradition. This shift is largely due to the number of popular Christian artists who attend the Presbyterian Church of America (PCA)–affiliated Christ Community Church in Franklin, Tennessee. The fact that 25 percent of the artists surveyed chose "nondenominational" as descriptive of their faith tradition is instructive in that it shows the continuing impact of the early suspicion toward institutions. However, it does not directly substantiate a continuing charismatic influence. Only 5 percent of the artists polled aligned themselves with charismatic denominations such as Four Square or Assemblies of God, and none of the artists chose to describe their faith tradition as charismatic. This is not surprising to me. For six years, starting in the early '80s, I attended two nondenominational charismatic churches. At neither church did we ever refer to ourselves first as charis-

matic. Our initial impulse was to emphasize that we were nondenominational. We might have added the qualifying terms "born again" or
"Spirit-filled."

5. See Melody Green, *No Compromise: The Life Story of Keith C*

8. Edwards, *Jonathan Edwards*, 89.

9. Edwards, *Jonathan Edwards*, 91.

10. Edwards, *Jonathan Edwards*, 91.

11. As a companion to Scripture in helping you sort out these issues for yourself, I recommend a book titled *Are Miraculous Gifts for Today? Four Views*
by Douglas Oss (Grand Rapids: Zondervan, 1996). This book, edited by
Wayne Grudem, includes arguments for and against the four main views
about the spiritual gifts that are prevalent today. While each argument is,
of course, biased, the editor leaves it up to readers to decide which view,
if any, is most faithful to Scripture.

12. Daniel G. Reid et al., eds., *Dictionary of Christianity in America: A Comprehensive Resource on the Religious Impulse That Shaped a Continent*
(Downers Grove: InterVarsity, 1990), 973.

13. John Fischer, quoted in April Hefner, "Don't Know Much 'bout History,"
CCM Magazine, April 1996, 40.

14. Fischer, quoted in Hefner, "Don't Know Much 'bout History."

Chapter 4: Of Baptists and Folk Musicals

1. All quotes attributed to Billy Ray Hearn, Ralph Carmichael, and Elwyn
Raymer are taken from interviews with the author, July 1997.

2. Joel Whitburn, *The Billboard Book of Top 40 Hits*, 6th ed. (New York: Billboard Publications, 1996).

Chapter 5: In Search of Theology

1. Richard Lovelace, *Dynamics of Spiritual Life: An Evangelical Theology of Renewal* (Downers Grove: InterVarsity, 1979), 29.

2. All quotes attributed to Wes King are taken from an interview with the author, *Gospel Music Week,* April 20-22, 1998.

3. J. I. Packer, *Hot Tub Religion: Christian Living in a Materialistic World* (Wheaton: Tyndale, 1987), 12.

4. Os Guinness, *The Gravedigger File* (Downers Grove: InterVarsity, 1983), 43.

5. Scott MacLeod, *Snakes in the Lobby* (Nashville: Provision Press, 1997), 44.

6. David F. Wells, *No Place for Truth: Or Whatever Happened to Evangelical Theology?* (Grand Rapids: Eerdmans, 1993), 290.

7. Shelley Breen, interview with the author, *Gospel Music Week,* April 20-22, 1998.

8. Mark Shaw, *10 Great Ideas from Church History: A Decision-Maker's Guide to Shaping Your Church* (Downers Grove: InterVarsity, 1997), 70.

Chapter 6: Music and Evangelism

1. Peter Furler, interview with the author, *Gospel Music Week,* April 20-22, 1998.

2. Phil Joel, interview with the author, *Gospel Music Week,* April 20-22, 1998.

3. Eddie Carswell, interview with the author, *Gospel Music Week,* April 20-22, 1998.

4. Member of Small Town Poets, interview with the author, *Gospel Music Week,* April 20-22, 1998.

5. Deborah Evans Price, Higher Ground, *Billboard,* June 7, 1997, 56.

6. William D. Romanowski, "Evangelicals and Popular Music: The Contemporary Christian Music Industry," *Religion and Popular Culture in America,* ed. Bruce David Forbes and Jeffrey H. Mahan (Berkeley: University of California Press, 2000), 113.

2. Brian Nelson, quoted in *CCM Update* 12, no. 3 (January 1998): 4.

3. Brian McSweeney, interview with the author, *Gospel Music Week,* April 20-22, 1998.

Chapter 9: The Ocean Too Big for the Glass

1. Charlie Peacock, "Monkeys at the Zoo," © 1994 Sparrow Song/Andi Beat Goes On Music, *Everything That's on My Mind,* © 1994 The Sparrow Corporation, Brentwood, TN. Used by permission.

2. Susie Luchsinger, interview with the author, *Gospel Music Week,* April 20-22, 1998.

3. Jim Fifield, quoted in April Hefner and Gregory Rumburg, "Buying into Family Values," *CCM Magazine* 19, no. 11 (May 1997): 52.

4. Phil Quartararo, quoted in Hefner and Rumburg, "Buying into Family Values."

Chapter 10: Stopping to Think

1. J. Alec Motyer, *The Prophecy of Isaiah: An Introduction and Commentary* (Downers Grove: InterVarsity, 1993), 452, 457.

2. Motyer, *The Prophecy of Isaiah,* 458.

3. Scott and Chris Dente, interview with the author, *Gospel Music Week,* April 20-22, 1998.

4. David F. Wells, *God in the Wasteland: The Reality of Truth in a World of Fading Dreams* (Grand Rapids: Eerdmans, 1994), 14.

5. Michael Wall, Bible Book Store/Solid Rock Christian Music and Video, Billings, Montana, correspondence with re:think/EMI, April 4, 1997. Used by permission.

Chapter 11: Truth and Consequences

1. Awards and Criteria Committee, Gospel Music Association (GMA) Board of Directors, letter to the author, September 24, 1997.

2. Awards and Criteria Committee, letter to the author, September 24, 1997.

Chapter 12: Worship: Stewardship of the Musical Praise Response

1. Dan Haseltine, quoted in Andy Argyrakis, "Story Behind the Song: Jars of Clay's 'Show You Love,' " *CCM Magazine* 26, no. 10 (April 2004): 13.

Chapter 13: Contemporary Christian Music and the World

1. Steven John Camp, "A Call for Reformation in the Contemporary Christian Music Industry," letter to CCM industry, October 31, 1997, www.worship.com/steve_camp_107_theses.htm.

2. John Seel, *The Evangelical Forfeit: Can We Recover?* (Grand Rapids: Baker, 1993), 110.

3. All quotes attributed to members of Reality Check are taken from an interview with the author, *Gospel Music Week*, April 20-22, 1998.

4. Os Guinness, *No God but God* (Chicago: Moody Press, 1992), 162.

5. Dick Keyes, *The Biblical Perspective of Ambition*, audiotape 2, no. 2311 and 2312. Available from Sound Word Associates, PO Box 2035, Mall Station, Michigan City, IN 46360.

6. Os Guinness, *The Call* (Nashville: Word, 1998), 178.

7. Guinness, *The Call*, 179.

8. David F. Wells, *No Place for Truth* (Grand Rapids: Eerdmans, 1993), 288.

9. Frank Breeden, quoted in "Plans Forming for 1998 Doves, Gospel Music Week," *CCM Update* 11, no. 39 (October 1997).

10. Naomi Judd, quoted in Jay Orr and Rick de Yampert, "Dove Goes to

13. Alister McGrath, *The Mystery of the Cross* (Grand Rapids: Zondervan, 1988), 161.

14. Shaw, *10 Great Ideas,* 32.

15. Alister McGrath, *Luther's Theology of the Cross: Martin Luther's Theological Breakthrough* (Oxford: Blackwell, 1985), 181.

16. David F. Wells, *God in the Wasteland* (Grand Rapids: Eerdmans, 1994), 40.

17. Dorothy Sayers, *The Man Born to Be King* (Grand Rapids: Eerdmans, n.d.), 35, quoted in Philip Yancey, *The Jesus I Never Knew* (Grand Rapids: Zondervan, 1995), 76.

18. Yancey, *The Jesus I Never Knew,* 81, quoting Helmut Thielicke, *Our Heavenly Father* (Grand Rapids: Baker 1974), 123.

19. Neil Postman, *Technology: The Surrender of Culture to Technology* (New York: Vintage, 1993), 13.

Chapter 14: Capitalism, the Corporation, and the Record Company

1. Melody Green, *No Compromise. The Life Story of Keith Green,* ed. David Hazard (Chatsworth: Sparrow Press, 1989), 230.

2. Green, *No Compromise,* 230.

3. Green, *No Compromise,* 229, 230.

4. Green, *No Compromise,* 268.

5. Green, *No Compromise,* 268.
6. David F. Wells, *God in the Wasteland* (Grand Rapids: Eerdmans, 1994), 50.
7. Wells, *God in the Wasteland,* 50.
8. Wells, *God in the Wasteland,* 50.
9. All quotes attributed to Don Weir are taken from an interview with the author, January 23, 1998.

Chapter 15: A Grander Vision

1. Shawn Young, e-mail correspondence, April 24, 2004. Used by permission.
2. Matt Odmark, interview with the author, *Gospel Music Week,* April 20-22, 1998.
3. Charlie Peacock-Ashworth, *New Way to Be Human: A Provocative Look at What It Means to Follow Jesus* (Colorado Springs: Shaw Books, 2004), xiv.

About the Authors

...spel Music Association's Dove Award for Producer of the Year. He has written such popular songs as Amy Grant's "Every Heartbeat" and dc Talk's "In the Light." He is the founder of the Art House, a study center dedicated to examining the artful life, and has contributed commentary and opinion to numerous radio shows, newspapers, and periodicals. Charlie and his wife, Andi Ashworth, live in Nashville, Tennessee. They have two grown children and one grandchild.

MOLLY NICHOLAS is Charlie Peacock's daughter and a graduate of Vanderbilt University. She works in development for a public broadcasting station and lives in Nashville with her husband, Mark, who is an author and music industry executive.

Charlie Peacock asks...
Are you living the life you're meant to live?

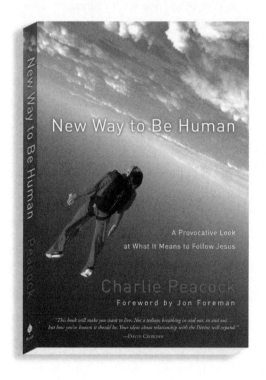

I f you're tired of faking it and are eager to stumble after Jesus with passion and authenticity, it's time for *New Way to Be Human*. With artful and inspiring words, award-winning recording artist and producer Charlie Peacock gives you a fresh, artful look at what it means to follow Jesus.

 SHAW BOOKS